Start Your Own

GIFT BASKET BUSINESS AND MORE

Additional titles in *Entrepreneur's* **Startup Series**

Start Your Own

Bed & Breakfast

Business on eBay

Business Support Service

Car Wash

Child Care Service

Cleaning Service

Clothing Store

Coin-Operated Laundry

Consulting Business

Crafts Business

E-Business

E-Learning Business

Event Planning Business

Executive Recruiting Service

Freight Brokerage Business

*Growing and Selling Herbs
    and Herbal Products*

Home Inspection Service

Import/Export Business

Information Consultant Business

Law Practice

Lawn Care Business

Mail Order Business

Medical Claims Billing Service

Personal Concierge Service

Personal Training Business

Pet-Sitting Business

*Restaurant and Five Other
    Food Businesses*

Self-Publishing Business

Seminar Production Business

Specialty Travel & Tour Business

Staffing Service

Successful Retail Business

Vending Business

Wedding Consultant Business

Wholesale Distribution Business

Entrepreneur
MAGAZINE'S

startup

2ND EDITION

Start Your Own

GIFT BASKET BUSINESS AND MORE

Special Events • Holiday
Real Estate • Corporate

Entrepreneur Press and Cheryl Kimball

EP
Entrepreneur.
Press

Jere L. Calmes, Publisher

Managing Editor: Marla Markman

Cover Design: Beth Hansen-Winter

Production and Composition: Alicen Armstrong Brown

This publication is designed to provide accurate and authoritative information in regard to the subject matter covered. It is sold with the understanding that the publisher is not engaged in rendering legal, accounting, or other professional services. If legal advice or other expert assistance is required, the services of a competent professional person should be sought.

Library of Congress Cataloging-in-Publication Data

Start your own gift basket business/by Entrepreneur Press and Cheryl Kimball.–2nd ed.
    p. cm.–(Start your own series)
  Includes index.
  ISBN-13: 978-1-59918-187-5 (alk. paper)
  ISBN-10: 1-59918-187-8
  1. Gift basket industry–Management. 2. Gift baskets. 3. New business enterprises–Management. 4. Home-based businesses–Management. I. Kimball, Cheryl.
II. Entrepreneur Press.

HD9999.G492S73 2008
745.59–dc22   2008004942

Printed in Canada

12 11 10 09 08   10 9 8 7 6 5 4 3 2 1

Contents

Preface xi

Chapter 1

More than One Basket:
A Look at the Gift Basket Business 1

It's All in the Presentation. 3
From Amateur to Pro 4
What Do You Need to Get Started? 4
Best Practices for Small Businesses. 5
Startup Stories 6
Fighting Failure 8

Chapter 2

Operations: It's Not Brain Surgery,
but It Takes Some Skill 11

Marketing 12
General Management and Administration. 12
Production. 12
Taking Orders 13
Purchasing 13

Billing. 15
The Outsourcing Resource. 15
You'll Design More than Baskets 16
Market Details. 16
Customer Profile and Order Information 17

Chapter 3

Defining Your Market. **21**
Market Research 22
Individual Buyers. 22
Business Customers 23
Getting in the Door 23
The Appointment 23
Phone Sales 24
Avoid Overlap 24
Showcase Your Baskets 24
Choosing a Niche 24
Developing a Product Line. 26
Types of Baskets. 26
Niche Market Worksheet 27
Know Thy Enemy. 28
Are You on a Mission? 29
Market Research Survey 31
Mission Statement Worksheet 32

Chapter 4

Structuring Your Business **33**
Naming Your Company 34
Trademarks. 36
Protect Your Mark. 37
Legal Structure 37
Licenses and Permits. 38
Business Insurance. 40
Professional Services 41
Create Your Own Advisory Board 43
Shipping and Receiving. 45
Shipping Supplies 46
Incoming 46

Chapter 5

Finances: Keep the Cash Flowing **47**

   Creating a Business Plan 48

      An Overview 48

      Business Logistics 49

      Market and Marketing 49

      Your Background 49

      Business Structure 49

      The Numbers 50

      SWOT Analysis 50

   Sources of Startup Funds 51

   How Much Do You Need? 52

   Turning Pro 54

   Estimated Startup Expenses 57

   Startup Expenses Worksheet 59

Chapter 6

Where Will You Start?

Locating and Setting Up Your Business **61**

   Going Retail 62

   Additional Retail Options 67

   Playing and Working Fair 68

   The Home Advantage 69

   Mail Order 70

      Your Primary Sales Tool 71

      The All-Important Mailing List 71

      Packing and Shipping Tips 72

   The Useful Website 72

   Nonretail Commercial Space 73

   Consignment Sales 73

   Displaying Merchandise 74

   Getting Ready to Work 75

   Should You Buy an Existing Operation? 76

   Business Opportunity or Franchise 77

      What Is a Franchise? 77

      Franchise Pros 78

      Franchise Cons 79

      What Is a Business Opportunity? 80

Chapter 7

Human Resources: The People Side of Your Company 81

Look in the Right Places 83

Evaluating Applicants 84

Once They're on Board 85

Employee Benefits 87

The Legal Side of Employees 87

Chapter 8

Equipping Your Business 89

Basic Office Equipment 90

Telecommunications 92

Other Equipment 94

Basket-Assembling Equipment 95

Equipment Checklist 96

Inventory 98

Sample: Cost of Goods Sold—Merchandiser 99

Trade Show Tips 102

Inventory Checklist 103

Inventory Control 103

Basic Stock 104

Lead Times 104

Excess Inventory 105

Tracking Inventory 105

Vehicles 106

Security 107

Chapter 9

Marketing Your Business 109

The Marketing Plan 110

Make Customer Service a Marketing Tool 111

Get Lost 111

Give Baskets Away 111

Reward Referrals 112

Cold Call 112

Market to Basket Recipients 113

Make Yourself Visible 114

Target Lesser-Known Holidays 115

Advertising 115
Trade Shows 116
Public Relations and Promotions 119

Chapter 10

Selling in Cyberspace **121**
Setting Up a Website 122
Website Design 123
Your Homepage 123
Drilling Down 124
The Rest of the Site 124
Selling from a Website 125
Shopping Cart 125
Payment Options 126
Other Ways to Sell Online 126
eBay 126
Other Sites 127
Trades 127
Marketing Your Website 127
E-Newsletters 128
Keep 'Em Interested 129
Don't Avoid Cyberspace 130

Chapter 11

Financial Management **131**
Key Financial Statements 132
Profit and Loss Statement 132
Balance Sheet 132
Cash-Flow Statement 133
Record Keeping 133
Billing 133
Setting Credit Policies 134
Red Flags 135
Accepting Credit and Debit Cards 136
Dealing with Your Own Creditors 137
Income Statement 138
Sample Credit Application 139

Chapter 12

Tales from the Trenches

Tales from the Trenches. 141
    Take Yourself and Your Business Seriously. 142
    Give Yourself a Boost When You Need It 142
    Keep Learning. 142
    Be Accessible 143
    Take Their Breath Away 143
    Market Your Business Constantly. 144
    Don't Market by Price. 144
    Stay Focused and Organized. 144
    Enhance Your Gift Basket Service with Extras. 144
    Guarantee Your Work 145
    Get Feedback. 145
    Establish and Maintain Flawless Credit 145
    Trade and Barter Whenever Possible 145
    Play by the Rules 145

Appendix A
    Gift Basket Business Resources. 147

Appendix B
    Naming Worksheet 151

Appendix C
    Checklists. 153

Appendix D
    Financial Worksheets. 165

Appendix E
    Business Strategy Forms 175

Appendix F
    Self-Assessment 179

Glossary 183

Index 189

Preface

Gift baskets could well be the closest thing to the perfect gift. They can be totally customized to suit the giver, the recipient, the occasion, and the desired price. For some people, creating them is the perfect business. Baskets represent an opportunity to be artistic, creative, and entrepreneurial.

Certainly it's an industry with tremendous "fun" potential. You get to buy lots of cute, clever gift items; you get to pull those items together in an attractive container and create a charming presentation; and you get to provide a product that delivers infinite pleasure to the recipient. Both givers and receivers of gift baskets appreciate the creativity and uniqueness of the concept.

There's also a respectable profit potential. As popular as they are, the market for gift baskets is still wide open and the sales opportunities are virtually limitless. As Dana S., who started Gift Baskets by Your Design seven years ago, says, "You can make a lot of money in this business!"

And it is not a game; the gift basket business is definitely serious business. While it doesn't require a great deal of startup capital—many successful gift basket businesses started with just a few hundred dollars—it does require thoughtful planning, preparation, and commitment fueled by a strong dose of excitement and enthusiasm.

This book is going to tell you everything you need to know to start and run a successful gift basket business. You will learn to:

- Identify a target market
- Develop an effective marketing plan
- Find and build relationships with suppliers
- Manage the administrative side of the business, including recordkeeping, billing, taxes, and insurance
- Design a plan to build the business you want to have, whether it's part time or full-time, homebased or in a commercial location, with employees or without
- Use the internet and a web site to get the most out of your sales potential

Because the best information about business comes from the people who are already in the trenches, we interviewed successful gift basket business owners who were happy to share their stories. These basketeers come from all over the country; some are homebased, some have retail operations; some are small and want to stay that way, some are large and growing; some do standard baskets, some do custom designs—but they all have valuable advice and information you will be able to learn and profit from. Throughout the book and in the last chapters with more "tales from the trenches," you will read about what works—and doesn't—for these folks, and how you can use their techniques in your own business.

You'll also learn what the gift basket business is really like. The hours can be flexible, but sometimes they're incredibly long—like at the holidays or any time when you get a call in the evening from someone who needs a basket first thing in the morning. The profit margins are excellent, but only if you're paying attention to detail and remembering to charge for everything, including your time and other less visible expenses. The market is tremendous, but you'll have a substantial amount of competition—directly from other gift basket businesses as well as from other general gift businesses—which means you need a plan to set yourself apart. The opportunity to express yourself creatively is virtually limitless, although sometimes you'll have to just do what the customer asks—even if it's not your preference.

Like anything else, there's no magic formula, no quick path to success. Your gift basket business will definitely not be a get-rich-quick operation. But it can be a substantial revenue generator for you.

We designed this book to be logical, informative, as well as entertaining, just like the gift basket business itself. In fact, the only thing that's dry about gift baskets is the dried flowers you'll occasionally use to decorate your creations. Just one word of warning: Take the time to sit back and relax as you read this book—because once your gift basket business is up and running, you're going to be a very busy person!

That's what Dana S. likes the least about the business: "There aren't enough hours in the day." But she has found a happy medium working on baskets in the mornings and spending the afternoons with her four children.

What does Dana like the best about the gift basket business? "It's a happy business. Even if you are delivering a sympathy basket. The first one I did, I felt terrible. I hand delivered it and I found that even in the worst, saddest situation, I had made someone happy for a minute."

Be prepared to learn about one of the most diverse—and happiest—businesses out there!

More than One Basket
A Look at the Gift Basket Business

Although gift baskets continue to be a hot business, with steady growth expected to continue well into the foreseeable future, they're not at all new. In fact, gift baskets have been a traditional form of gift giving ever since humans figured out how to weave baskets. Throughout history, baskets filled with fruit, nuts, wild game, and other foodstuff, flowers, and other material tokens have been presented as a sign of affection or a gesture of goodwill. The contents could be consumed, and the container then used for cooking, storing, and transporting food, or for some other practical or decorative purpose. Or, in today's parlance, they could be "regifted," as a gift basket filled with new goodies and given to someone else. It was a gift that had great value and essentially no waste.

Today, gift baskets are equally practical and infinitely more creative. They run the gamut from traditional Easter-style "goodie" baskets to baskets made especially for golfers, chocolate lovers, new homeowners, and brides-to-be. Some people focus almost exclusively on the contents, others see the basket (or other container) as a very important part of the gift. In fact, a growing number of gift baskets aren't baskets at all—they're boxes, fruit crates, tote bags, hats, ceramic pots, mixing bowls, buckets, and more, all filled with food, gifts, and other collectible items designed to delight the recipient.

So who buys gift baskets and why? Just about everyone for every imaginable occasion. They buy premade baskets by occasion or theme, or baskets specially designed for a specific individual. They buy baskets from large chain stores, small specialty shops, and homebased basket makers—and they'll buy them from you.

The market for gift baskets is great, and as long as people buy each other presents, you'll have a steady stream of customers. You have a product that is in high demand and that people are familiar with. You don't need to convince anyone that they should buy gift baskets—you just need to let them know you are their best source, and that you can deliver the product they need when they need it. One 13-year veteran in the business told us she believes the industry is in its infancy, with the real growth yet to be experienced. In recent years, that growth has been spurred by the internet.

Your revenue will be limited only by how hard you want to work and how much you want your business to grow. You can easily gross $10,000 or more annually working part time from home, or $1 million and up operating a retail store or mail order business full time.

About half of your business will be holiday-based, and the majority of that will be Christmas-related. One of the fastest-growing segments of the gift basket industry is corporate holiday orders. When the Christmas rush is over, Valentine's Day, Easter, Mother's Day, Thanksgiving, and Secretaries' Day are the most profitable holidays.

Most gift basket business owners see holidays as both a blessing and a curse. They can earn a lot of money making holiday baskets, but they have to work very hard during times of the year when they might prefer to do other things. This is something to keep in mind as you consider starting a gift basket business.

The bottom line on making gift baskets is that it's a highly creative and gratifying occupation. It features all the best aspects of hands-on work, design, coordinating, planning, and customer service. Your product is something you take pleasure in making, your customers enjoy buying, and the recipients are delighted to receive. And only you can set the limits as to how creative you want to be.

It's All in the Presentation

All of the elements of a gift basket—from the container to the contents, to the ribbons and the wrapping—can be fun and lively, but they require knowledge and skill to put everything together. Not all baskets have to be glitzy and glamorous; they just need to fit the tastes of your customers, and live up to the expectations you have set.

This is a highly creative enterprise, requiring a good eye for color, balance, texture, and thematic coordination. If the finished product doesn't excite, delight, and sell itself, nothing else you can do will make the business work.

Certainly this is not to say that making gift baskets is as exacting an art as oil painting or wood carving, but it is more difficult than it looks. Before you make a major investment in equipment or materials, test your ability to actually make the baskets. Shop around for some simple materials such as baskets, tissue paper, ribbons, gourmet foods, dried flowers, perfumed soaps, etc. Get just enough materials and supplies to make two or three complete baskets, then experiment with putting the baskets together. Compare your finished product to baskets you may have received or seen in stores. Does yours have a creative flair? Does it have an air of having been professionally assembled? Be brutally honest—would someone be willing to pay for the basket and be proud to give it as a gift?

Perfect Gifts

Gift baskets are the perfect gift for:

- ❍ Valentine's Day
- ❍ Mother's Day
- ❍ Father's Day
- ❍ Easter
- ❍ Halloween
- ❍ Thanksgiving
- ❍ Christmas
- ❍ New home
- ❍ Baby shower
- ❍ New pet
- ❍ Bridal shower
- ❍ Wedding
- ❍ Get well
- ❍ Sympathy
- ❍ Hostess gift
- ❍ Graduation
- ❍ Going away
- ❍ Job promotion
- ❍ Thank you
- ❍ Birthday
- ❍ Hannukah
- ❍ Celebrations of all kinds

It's perfectly OK to copy ideas from other gift basket makers, especially when you are just getting started in your venture. Don't worry, you'll get more creative as you go along. But, what's as important as creativity is the overall visual impact of the basket—the items need to be attractively and carefully arranged for the maximum effect.

From Amateur to Pro

You may be considering a gift basket business because you're already making gift baskets and giving them to friends and family members. While turning a hobby into a business is an excellent way to get started, it's not as easy as it may seem.

The biggest question is this: Your friends and family may ooh and ahh over baskets you give them, but when it gets down to the real bottom line, will they take out their checkbooks and pay you to make more?

Keep in mind that if you make gift baskets as a hobby or to give them as personal gifts, you can make them when you feel like it—and if you don't feel like it, there are no serious consequences to just not doing anything. When you're in business, things change. Customers depend on you. Think about how you would feel if you ordered a gift for a special occasion and it was either late or didn't arrive at all—or arrived on time, but wasn't what you ordered. As a business owner who is being paid to make baskets, the buck stops with you. It doesn't matter that there's something else you'd rather do, or that you're not in the mood, or that your stock order didn't arrive on time—your customers are counting on you, and you have to deliver.

If you're up to that, keep reading.

What Do You Need to Get Started?

One of the more appealing things about the gift basket industry is that you can start small with a minimal amount of equipment and increase the sophistication of your operation as your business grows and generates revenue. Or, if you have the cash and resources, you can start big and grow faster.

More important than money and materials is the reality that you need physical stamina. This is a physically demanding business. You don't have to be extraordinarily strong, but be aware that you'll spend hours standing at your assembly table, bending, stretching, lifting, packing, and carrying. You'll spend even more hours getting in and out of your vehicle, walking, and carrying as you make deliveries and sales calls. When you do get to sit down, you'll be on the phone, at your computer, or doing other paperwork. For all its fun and creativity, making gift baskets and serving customers is hard work. It demands energy, physical and emotional fortitude, persistence, and perseverance.

The actual equipment you need is detailed in Chapter 8, but with the right attitude and information, you can start your business with little more than a few baskets and a good pair of scissors. Of course, it helps to have a few additional items, and we recommend that you do, but don't let limited resources stop you from pursuing your dream. Gift basket business owners have started with as little as $300, and others were able to invest $20,000 to $30,000 upfront. They all agree that what counts is a basic understanding of the business and a willingness to do whatever it takes to keep your customers happy—that's all you really need in the way of "startup capital."

One of the main factors in the complexity of your startup expenses is whether you decide to have a storefront or not.

Best Practices for Small Businesses

When running a small business, there are several "best practices" that will help your business lean in the direction of success. Here are six:

1. *Give money the respect it deserves.* You do not have to be embarrassed about making money and you should not be shy about collecting it. Unless you are set up as a nonprofit (no easy task), no customer should expect a business to be unprofitable. Set your fees at a rate the market will bear and that will bring you the cash flow you need to create and maintain a good business. Give this little service away or that half hour of time consulting on the phone for free and you are eating away at what time you have for your paying customers.

2. *Create a business plan, no matter how small your business startup will be.* A business plan gives you a guide to base all decisions on and against which to measure your success and plan for the future.

3. *Borrow as little as possible but as much as you need.* Undercapitalization is a big reason for small businesses' failures. You need to be able to keep your business

running in order to get customers to bring in revenue and make your business a financial success. Two of your most substantial expenses in starting up a gift basket business will be inventory and, if you have a retail operation, your rent. Learn to be discerning in your purchasing. Products can be obtained quickly these days, and there isn't much need to keep a lot in stock, especially if you make baskets that contain perishables. Be realistic about what you need for a storefront, and be creative in making it look exactly as you want it to even if you can't afford that exact downtown, riverfront location you covet.

4. *Maintain health insurance.* If your spouse has a job that provides benefits to you, awesome. But don't be without at least catastrophic insurance that would cover large hospital and emergency bills. If at all possible—although it's not easy for small-business owners—also maintain a disability policy that provides some level of coverage if you are injured and cannot perform the type of work that you do. This is typically quite expensive and probably isn't necessary if your income isn't needed by your family. But if it is, do some research and find a policy.

5. *Be realistic about how much business you can take on.* Burnout is another top factor in why small businesses close—the owner/manager simply wears out! This often happens within the first 18 months. While this is not to say that any small-business owner can afford to be accused of being lazy, committing 18 hours/day, 6 or 7 days a week, is exhausting, plain and simple. If your plan is to start up your business, make it phenomenally successful, and sell out within 2 years, perhaps this approach will work. But if you are planning to be in it for the long haul, building up gradually and perhaps selling in 10 to 15 years, start slowly and increase your business in a logical way.

6. *Hire employees sparingly.* Employees' paychecks as well as contributions for social security, workers' compensation, and unemployment taxes add up fast. When you think you need an employee, do a thorough financial breakdown, preferably with your accountant, and make sure the employee will pay for himself or herself either through increased or more efficient business in a relatively short time, say six months. Do thorough interviews and get references from any potential employee so it doesn't become a nightmare.

Startup Stories

Is there such a thing as a "typical" gift basket business owner? Well, most of these entrepreneurs are typically hardworking, creative, and committed to their business—but beyond that, there are no consistent similarities. The differences begin with what motivates the startup of the business and end with how the company is operated. In fact, when we asked gift basket business owners around the country how they got started, no two told the same story.

Fifteen years ago, Sue C., a gift basket maker in Salt Lake City, Utah, found herself out of a job when the company she'd been working for closed its doors. Her search for a job with a retail florist was futile because prospective employers felt she was overqualified. So with her final paycheck of $300, she started her own gift basket business in her home.

Stat Fact
According to *Gift Basket Review* magazine, the typical gift basket business is nearly 16 years old and a full-time enterprise for its owners.

"I knew what I wanted to do, so I wrote a business plan, got all the proper licensing, bought some stationery, and joined the chamber of commerce," Sue recalls. "My first order was for a $35 gift basket, and I had to wait until that money came in to buy products for the next basket." She's outgrown her home space and now operates from a warehouse.

Christine M. was an executive with a cosmetics company who enjoyed creating baskets as gifts for her friends. She was also totally unimpressed with the commercial baskets available in upscale department stores and amazed at how popular they were. "I used to sit in a department store and watch people flock over to these things that looked horrendous, but they loved them," Christine says. "I thought that if they were going crazy over that, imagine what they would do with something that was put together nicely." And that's what convinced her that a gift basket business would work, so she founded a profitable homebased gift basket business.

Chris K. got the idea to start her own homebased gift basket business after her mother-in-law passed away. The family received a number of gift baskets containing food—but so much of it was perishable that it ended up spoiling and being thrown out. "My cousin and I were talking about this, and she said there should be something in the baskets to keep long term. So we got the idea that if we put in gifts—real, true gifts, not just food and perishable items—the basket would be more memorable for both the recipient and the giver," Chris says. It didn't take long for the two cousins to establish a formal partnership, develop a business plan, and get their business up and running.

Fun Fact
One of the major appeals of gift baskets is the fact that the contents can be consumed and yet the "gift wrap" (the basket or other container) remains a wonderful keepsake.

How long will it take you? That depends, of course, on your own circumstances. There's no serious rush—this is an industry still in its infancy, thriving but with a huge potential market still untapped. So settle down for some reading that we hope you'll find both informative and entertaining—and that will catapult you into the exciting, profitable, and fun world of gift baskets.

Fighting Failure

A discussion of starting a small business can't take place without discussing the possibility of failure. According to the Small Business Administration, one-third of small businesses close after two years, half after four years, and 60 percent after six years.

There are lots of reasons for small-business failure. The main ones are the following long list:

- Running out of money
- Lack of business planning
- Inefficient cost, quality, and/or inventory control
- Underpricing of goods sold
- Poor customer relations
- Failure to promote and maintain a favorable public image
- Bad relations with suppliers
- Bad management
- Loss of key personnel (illness, quitting)
- Reluctance to seek professional help
- Poor tax planning
- Inadequate insurance
- Lack of staff training
- Insufficient knowledge of the industry
- Inability to compete
- Failure to anticipate market trends
- Inadequate cash-flow control
- Growth without adequate capitalization
- Ignoring data on the company's financial position
- Incomplete financial records
- Overextending credit
- Overborrowing
- Overdue receivables
- Excessive demands from creditors

Rent increases, and many other factors, and it's a wonder any business opens at all! But they do. And many survive. The way they survive is to avoid the pitfalls mentioned above by planning carefully.

Burnout is another factor leading to the closing of many businesses. While it is critical to plan to work hard, all work and no play does make the business owner too exhausted to take care of her business properly. No one is able to sustain an 80-hour work week without beginning to lose enthusiasm. And if anyone needs to be enthusiastic about your business, it's you! It's important to be sharp enough to be creative, especially in a business like making gift baskets.

Starting a business is a long process. Give yourself plenty of time—as much as six months to a year—to do the necessary research for your business plan.

Work for someone else to learn more about the gift business in general, or gift baskets in particular. Talk with other business owners. Take courses to shore up your management skills. Investing in yourself before making one of the biggest investments you will ever make will increase your odds of success. Research and planning can help prevent potential disasters like running out of money, making the wrong hiring decisions, not taking advantage of market opportunities, and/or choosing the wrong partner or wrong location.

Plan for success to avoid business failure!

Operations
It's Not Brain Surgery, but It Takes Some Skill

What will it be like once you're in business? We asked several gift basket business owners to tell us about their days—and no two days are exactly alike.

Most retail gift basket businesses open anywhere from 8 to 11 in the morning and close sometime between 4 and 9 in the evening. Homebased operations have more flexibility with hours; in a retail operation, having the store open and ready to serve customers during your posted hours is essential. The hours you post should be in line with when customers are likely to come in. How you organize your day depends on the specific nature of your business and your own personal working style, but each day will likely consist of a diversity of tasks: some administrative work, marketing, order taking, purchasing, billing, making deliveries, and, of course, designing and assembling gift baskets.

These functions will be addressed in more detail in later chapters, but the following observations have been gathered from asking successful basketeers about their typical day.

Marketing

Marketing is an ongoing process of finding new customers and building relationships with the ones you have. It's a lot like brushing your teeth—you have to do it regularly and thoroughly to be effective. Your marketing efforts should permeate absolutely everything you do.

General Management and Administration

Though the focus of any business is the product or service that generates revenue, you still need to manage and administer the processes that get your product or service to the marketplace. Proper attention to detail in this area often spells the difference between success and failure—even for a basketeer whose creations are stunning.

If you have a retail store, this will include all aspects of keeping that store running smoothly. Little things like being open during the times you advertise you are open are crucial—potential customers forget you even exist if they finally have a moment to drop in your shop and there's a note on the door saying you'll be back in a half hour. Few people have a half hour to spare to wait to do business with you.

Make sure if you have employees everyone knows what is important to you to help you put your best foot forward for customers and potential customers.

Production

This is the really fun part of the gift basket business—and it's probably what attracted you to it in the first place. But as much as you enjoy it, it's no longer something you do exclusively for pleasure. Basket production is a critical part of your company. It must be done to your high standards, as well as the customer's specifications, on a schedule that will allow you to meet your delivery commitments. Many basketeers—especially homebased, solo operators—put in long hours at the production table. Chris K. remembers her first large corporate order: The customer wanted to present wine and cheese baskets to its employees at the company Christmas dinner.

The last-minute order literally took Chris all night—she finished at about 7 A.M., in plenty of time for the customer to pick them up at 9 A.M. When you are establishing your business, you need to do what's necessary to take advantage of large orders.

Taking Orders

Especially if you make custom baskets, a big part of your day will be spent talking to customers as you take their orders. A system to expedite this process will not only save you time, but make sure you get all the information you need. Consider developing a checklist of questions that will identify both mandatory and optional information (see the sample "Customer Profile and Order Information" on page 17). This can be done either on paper or using a computer database, whichever is easier for you. What's important is that you get sufficient information to let you create a basket that is truly customized, perfect for each recipient, and exactly what the customer ordered. Repeat customers will be impressed if you can readily call up the details of their last order.

Purchasing

If you like shopping for clever and unusual items, this is a great business to be in. But buying for a business is more than just shopping. Building and maintaining supplier relationships is a critical part of the gift basket business. Find suppliers that are willing to work with you when you're small, then be loyal to them as you grow. And you must always consider costs; no business stays in business unless there are profits generated to keep the business running.

Never buy a product unless you've seen a sample of it. Most suppliers are willing to send free samples; some may ask you to pay for the sample. It's worth paying a small amount to check something out rather than buying a large quantity and finding out the quality isn't up to your standards.

Going Steady

When Yvette L. started her gift basket business, she enjoyed the creative process of designing and assembling baskets, but she knew that even in this industry, there needed to be more than just a series of special occasions. Her startup strategy included looking for a source of steady income, so she focused on apartment complexes.

Large apartment complexes always have someone moving in or out, and many will give new tenants a welcome basket when they sign their lease. Others send baskets to tenants who renew their leases. And some even send tenants baskets on their birthdays or other special events.

To tap this market of year-round revenue, Yvette systematically called on complexes in specific geographic areas. She made a personal visit to the manager with a sample of the basket. "I scheduled the presentations in the same area, and made a presentation to somebody new every 15 minutes," she says. "Not everyone said yes. But I was enthusiastic and excited. I believed in what I was doing. I thought it would work, and it did."

She came up with an affordable design (a paper plate holder with coffee and cookies, wrapped in cellophane and tied with a bow) that she could profitably sell at $5. She organized her client apartment complexes regionally, assigning them a day of the week to order, and a day she would deliver. The night before their order day, she sent a fax reminding them to tally up how many move-in and thank-you baskets they would need. She called the next day for the order, which often included a request for a different type of basket.

"I didn't put any pressure on them—they either needed something or they didn't," Yvette says. But when they did need something—either the routine baskets or something special—they had a relationship with her, and she knew she could count on their business.

In addition to samples, ask for two copies of the supplier's brochure or catalog. Why two? A gift basket consultant explains: "You want one to keep in the office that you can make notes on, and one to take with you on presentations to show people what kinds of items you can get to go in their baskets. You want to be able to write prices and other information on your file copy, but you don't want customers to see those notes, or know what you're paying for a product."

Set boundaries with manufacturers' representatives. Don't let them pressure you into buying larger quantities than you need—make your decisions based on your business strategy, not on the salesperson's desire to make a big commission. Even if there is a substantially better discount for buying 100 opposed to 60, if you sell only 55, your increased discount got you nowhere. You know your business better than the sales rep does.

Also, insist that salespeople respect your time by setting appointments to meet with you at off-peak times of the day and by focusing their presentations on items that are appropriate for your particular business. Remember that your first priority is to serve your customers and build your business. They should meet you at your convenience, not theirs.

"A lot of times, salespeople will call and say they will be in the area around 10 o'clock, and I'll tell them I can't see them until after 4," says Claire S., who owns a retail gift basket shop in Sunrise, Florida. "It's not fair to my customers to say that I can't see them for an hour because I'm sitting with a rep." As to succumbing to sales pressure, she says, "It's hard in the beginning, because you are so intimidated and you think you have to buy everything. But now if I see one or two items I like, I'll try them—but I don't feel like I have to buy everything they show me."

If you go on buying trips to trade shows and merchandise marts, learn to be cautious in your buying. What looks good in the midst of the excitement of a trade show may not look so great when you get back to the shop, and it will seem even worse if you have 10 cases of the item on their way to you.

> **Smart Tip**
> **Tip...**
>
> When designing a basket, never mix food and scented personal products. The vision of savoring gourmet chocolates in a tub filled with fragrant bubble bath might be delightful, but if the scented products can permeate (or worse yet leak into) everything else in your basket, including food items, your gift basket will be a flop.

Billing

The sale isn't complete until the money is in your bank account. Process your credit card charges before the basket goes out the door. Invoice promptly based on the terms you've agreed to extend to your customers.

Along with billing is processing your receivables. When checks come in, credit them to the appropriate account and get them in the bank as soon as possible. Your revenue should be working for your business ASAP.

The Outsourcing Resource

One of the hottest trends in business today is outsourcing—the practice of finding someone outside your company to provide a specific service or handle a specific task. Typical functions that might be outsourced include graphic design, accounting and bookkeeping, secretarial work, and web page design and maintenance. You might also want to outsource all or part of your marketing process.

A relatively new idea in the gift basket industry is to actually outsource your baskets. When Sharon M. started her mail order gift basket company in New York City in 1983, she made custom baskets herself. Today, her company doesn't make any baskets at all—all of the items in their catalog are outsourced to various suppliers who create the gifts and drop-ship directly to Sharon's customers.

Sharon says this is a trend that just makes sense. Typically, gift basket business owners do it all—marketing, purchasing, designing, assembling, packing, shipping, customer service, administration, and more. After operating that way for years—and very successfully—she decided to focus on what she does best, which is sales and marketing, and outsource the rest of the business. "We found really great sources around the country who can do the other end of our business," Sharon says. "We can really rely on these people. They do a great job; they are our teammates. We do the marketing, we take the orders, we fax the orders to them, and they ship them out directly to the customer under our name."

You may want to keep the basket design aspect for yourself and outsource another part of the business you don't enjoy or aren't as good at. The point is that outsourcing allows you to get help without adding costly employees.

Beware!
Never miss a basket delivery deadline; always get them out on time. If you have to let something slide, it can be your administrative tasks, but never, ever fail to deliver a basket when promised.

You'll Design More than Baskets

Though the idea of designing gift baskets may be what attracted you to this business in the first place, you can see that you'll be creating far more than just baskets—you'll be designing an organization that will exist to make people happy. The first step is understanding who those people are. So let's take a look at your market.

Market Details

You market will in part be created by the types of baskets you choose to offer. If baskets with kids stuff is a large part of what you decide to do, your market will consist in large part of parents. If the baskets you offer are mainly of the romantic variety, chances are your market will consist of a lot of men looking to buy a romantic gift basket for their sweethearts. If you put together a line of baskets containing automotive accessories (hey, why not?), you will most likely be targeting a female buyer looking for something unique to give her guy.

Customer Profile and Order Information

(You can keep this electronically. If you use a simple database software, you can sort your customer by any field in the database and further make use of the information for special offers, etc.)

Mandatory Information

Customer (sender) name: _____

Address: _____

City, state, zip: _____

Phone: _____

Fax: _____

E-mail: _____ Website: _____

Billing information (credit card details or invoicing instructions): _____

_____

Message/signature on gift card: _____

_____

Budget: _____

Recipient's name: _____

Address: _____

Phone: _____

Delivery information (include special instructions, delivery deadline): _____

_____

Type of basket (include general description of contents): _____

_____

_____

Customer Profile and Order Information, continued

Optional Information to Assist In Creating a Customized Basket

Do you want the basket to have a full look, or do you prefer a quality rather than quantity style? _____

_____

_____

What style does the recipient prefer—country, contemporary, traditional, etc.?

_____

What are the recipient's favorite hobbies, sports, or other interests? _____

_____

What is the recipient's occupation? _____

_____

If the recipient(s) has children, list:

Name	Sex	Age	Special Interest
_____	___	___	_____
_____	___	___	_____
_____	___	___	_____
_____	___	___	_____
_____	___	___	_____

If the recipient(s) has pets, list:

Type of Pet	Name
_____	_____
_____	_____
_____	_____

Besides what you focus your baskets on, what type of products you put in them will have an impact on the demographic your market consists of. If you buy most of the items you put in your basket at the local dollar store, don't count on the executives at the local top financial institutions to be your market base. Likewise, if you make baskets that consist of high-end perfumes, silk scarves, and cashmere slippers, don't expect the local factory workers to be dishing out $350 for a gift basket.

So part of your market depends on what you want to be putting together for baskets. And when you figure out what market you want to put your efforts into attracting, then you need to be sure you can reach those buyers. There are lots of people willing to pay $350 for a gift basket, but you need to be sure a good supply of those people know you exist. You'll learn lots more about how to do that in Chapter 9, "Marketing Your Business."

Defining
Your Market

Just about everybody has the potential to become
your customer. But if you try to sell to the entire world, you will end
up not selling much at all. You need to research and identify a market, choose a niche, and then develop a plan to serve it.

The market for gift basket businesses is no longer
limited to a single consumer looking for a unique gift. At one time,
women made up the largest segment of the industry's market,

both as customers and basket recipients. But that situation is changing. The corporate sector is rapidly becoming a major purchaser of gift baskets, and for good reason.

Gift baskets have the advantage of being personal yet professional. They can be designed to fit the tastes of the recipient while also reflecting the personality of the giver and the nature of the circumstances that prompted the gift.

Gift baskets are also popular because they take the hassle of shopping out of gift buying. Whether they're buying for business or personal reasons, people today rarely have time to go out and hunt down the perfect gift—but they'd like the recipient to think they did just that. So they call a gift basket service, describe their ideas, price range, and recipient's preferences, and voila! They can have a custom-made gift sent without ever having to shop.

Market Research

Market research provides businesses with data that will allow them to identify and reach particular market segments and solve or avoid marketing problems. A thorough market survey forms the foundation of any successful business. It would be impossible to develop marketing strategies or an effective product line without market research.

The goal of market research is for you to identify your market, find out where it is, and develop a strategy to communicate with prospective customers in a way that will convince them to buy from you.

> **Bright Idea**
> If you know the basket recipient has a pet, add a box of appropriate animal treats to the basket. If you know the animal's name, write it on the box or attach a personalized gift tag. Animal lovers will be very impressed with your thoughtfulness and thoroughness.

The two primary gift basket markets are the individual gift-giver and the corporate client. Both can be lucrative and fun to serve.

Individual Buyers

The individual gift-giver is more likely to be a woman. This is because men may order a gift basket, but they typically only think of it after they've seen one. Women are more likely to have seen, sent, or received gift baskets. Therefore, they are better able to picture the basket they have in mind for someone even if they don't actually have one in front of them as they might in a retail store. Also, women are more likely to know that custom baskets make great gifts.

Another reason women buy more gift baskets than men is that wives, mothers, and girlfriends often assume the responsibility of buying gifts on behalf of the men in their lives, even when the recipient is the man's friends, relatives, or co-workers.

Gift basket buyers tend to be in the moderate- to upper-income levels, so your market research needs to include finding out where people in this particular demographic shop.

Business Customers

Corporate clients can be some of your best customers. Most businesses have long gift lists, plus they buy year-round, not just during the holidays. They regularly recognize employee anniversaries, promotions, retirements, and birthdays throughout the year. Many also give gifts to customers during the year.

Like individual gift buyers, business customers frequently don't have the time or personnel available to shop. A savvy gift basket business can function as a customer's personal shopper, so all the client has to do is make one phone call and a special gift is on the way.

Getting in the Door

One of the first things you need to do to be able to sell to corporate clients is get beyond the administrative guard to the executive who can make decisions. This process should not be rushed. The last thing you want is for the administrative person in charge of protecting the time of the executive to take a disliking of you!

Stat Fact

61 percent of gift basket business owners reported to *Gift Basket Review* magazine's 2006 survey that more than 51 percent of their business came from corporate customers. Of those, 43 percent rely on corporate giving for 70 percent or more of their annual business.

The best way to get on that person's better side is to be polite, efficient, and extremely organized. Don't get into schmooze mode; they can smell insincerity a mile away. Make sure the executive secretary knows what you want and how much of the executive's time you will need. Provide advance materials so the executive can make some pre-decisions on her or his own time before you meet.

The Appointment

When you do get that precious meeting time, use it wisely. Come prepared with sales materials that showcase the very best of what you can do. Also, come prepared with the ability to take an order. If you get the executive thinking creatively, you may well find she has an event the following week that could be just the right opportunity to use your gift basket services.

Phone Sales

Although gift baskets can be a bit cumbersome to ship, you will have researched the ways of making sure a basket arrives at its destination looking just as beautiful as when you packed it up. So don't be afraid to do some corporate selling over the phone to potential corporate customers outside your general area. Some good phone sales techniques include:

- *Create a selling mood.* You can set the tone of the conversation by making sure you come across as knowledgeable, friendly, helpful, and trustworthy. There is a big difference between face-to-face selling where other things help you project these images. On the phone you've got only your voice. Practice sounding confident and informed.

- *Prepare your sales pitch.* You may end up improvising based on where the conversation leads, but don't go into the call without a prepared sales script. But don't read it; memorize it so you don't sound like a machine. Be sure you are comfortable with every word in the script; practice at least out loud, perhaps even into a tape recorder.

- *Be assertive.* Don't end the conversation without having made sure the potential customer knows how your company can be helpful to him.

Avoid Overlap

Finally, unless you can really create distinctively different offerings, don't solicit corporate clients in the same industry. The executive of Big Giant Widgets wants her clients to remember her company as the one that sends out those lovely gift baskets after a sale.

Showcase Your Baskets

Lastly, showcase your wares! Send a nice thank-you-for-your-time basket to the executive you dealt with, especially if you met in person. And send a thank-you-for-your-cooperation basket to that all-important assistant who helped you get the appointment. Don't go over the top, something small is perfect, but make sure it is memorable, of the very best quality, and represents exactly what you want the potential client to remember about your business.

Choosing a Niche

There are a number of valid reasons for choosing a well-defined market niche. By targeting a specific market segment, you can tailor your product line, marketing efforts, and customer service system to meet that segment's needs. You'll have better control over your inventory because you'll need to stock fewer items. And you'll develop a reputation as an expert in your area—and that means you can charge more. Think about it: In the medical field, who earns more, a family practitioner or a neurosurgeon? The neurosurgeon, naturally, because she's a specialist and what she does requires greater skill. Of course, gift baskets don't require the skill of a neurosurgeon, or even a family doctor, but still, not everyone can create them. Position yourself as an expert in the type of gift baskets you want to make.

Once you've defined your market niche and determined what volume it will create, you need to analyze it to decide if it has the potential to generate the revenue and profits you want. This is a critical issue. You may, for example, want to target upscale customers, but realize you've defined a geographic area that does not include enough of those customers to support your business. In that case, you have two choices: You can either change the geographic area or you can change your strategy to also target middle- and lower-middle-income customers.

What is wrong with just going after anybody in the world who might ever want to buy a gift basket for any reason? That market segment includes literally millions of people, and it's impossible for any small business to communicate effectively with that many people. Can you afford to send even one piece of direct mail to one million prospective customers? Of course not. But when you narrow that market down to, for example, 500 or 1,000 customers in a particular area, doing a successful direct-mail campaign is much more affordable and manageable.

To help you define your niche, complete the "Niche Market Worksheet" on page 27.

Cornering the Corporate Market

If you're going to target the corporate market, you'll be more successful if you define what segment of this broad market you're after. Some ideas:

- ○ Health care
- ○ Employee gifts
- ○ Apartments
- ○ Corporate headquarters
- ○ Banks, mortgage companies, and other financial institutions
- ○ Real estate
- ○ Special event/promotional
- ○ Hotels and vacation resorts
- ○ Automobile dealerships

▲

Developing a Product Line

Having identified your market and determined what potential customers are likely to buy and how much they will spend, you need to decide on your standard basket offerings. Even though you may promote yourself as a custom basket maker, you need an internal structure of standard baskets to use as a guide for marketing and purchasing. Standard baskets can serve as samples you can show to prospective customers.

If the contents are nonperishable, they can be premade and stored. And since they're all the same, you can assemble a number of standard baskets fairly quickly, which lowers your labor costs and means you can charge lower prices for those selections.

Standard baskets should serve to showcase the quality of your offering and provide a basic basket that can be customized per your customer's needs. Dana Sonia of Gift Baskets by Your Design in New Hampshire chose to not offer any standard premade baskets, but made it part of her niche to completely customize. If a potential customer wants something premade, she refers them to other basket businesses.

Look in Appendix C for a checklist on pricing and in Appendix F for one on conducting a focus group.

Types of Baskets

The following baskets are standards in most lines:

- *Gourmet/food baskets.* These are the most popular of all gift baskets. Some will be based on a theme, such as a chocolate lover's basket, a tea time basket, or a pasta and sauce basket. Others will provide a varied arrangement of complementary items, such as fresh fruit, cheeses, crackers, cookies, specialty coffees, hot chocolate, fine mints, etc. When developing food baskets, consider the ethnic makeup of your market; for example, a kosher basket could be a consistently popular item.

- *Toiletry baskets.* These arrangements include lotions, bath oils, shampoos, perfumed soaps, facial masks, potpourris, and talcum powder. For originality and greater consumer appeal, further focus the theme by choosing all-natural products or those made by famous-name manufacturers.

- *Shower baskets.* Baskets for both wedding and baby showers are extremely popular and can be filled with any number of "necessities" for the upcoming change

> **Tip...**
>
> **Smart Tip**
> Keep the value of each basket and its various contents in proportion. For example, when a customer wants to pay $50 for a gift, don't use a basket that retails for $30 and then toss in $10 or $15 worth of contents. The customer will feel cheated, and you won't make any money.

Niche Market Worksheet

Have you defined your market niche well? How comfortably and clearly you can answer the following questions will let you know.

Who is my customer? _____

_____

Whom are they buying for? _____

_____

Where is my customer located? _____

_____

Where are the basket recipients located? _____

_____

What is their price range? _____

_____

How many baskets a year will they buy? _____

_____

_____

What particular style/type of basket do they buy? _____

_____

_____

How will I communicate with my prospective customers? _____

_____

_____

Will this market niche generate sufficient revenue for me to reach my income and profitability goals? _____

_____

in the recipient's life. A baby basket could contain baby shampoo, baby powder, a washcloth, bibs, rattles, pacifiers, and a special treat for Mom. A wedding basket could be romantic, filled with a book on love and marriage, perfume, bubble bath, fancy chocolates, champagne glasses, and a garter. Or it could be more practical, with a cookbook, dishtowels, kitchen utensils, and spices.

Most gift basket businesses offer a combination of standard and custom baskets. Custom baskets can be a made-from-scratch arrangement, or a variation on one of your standard offerings. A wonderful way to showcase a special gift—perhaps a family heirloom, photograph, or piece of jewelry—is to include it in a gift basket. You might trigger an idea if you mention this to the customer.

Consider offering anywhere from 6 to 20 standard baskets in a wide range of sizes and prices. For example, your chocolate lover's basket (a must for any gift basket business) may come in several sizes and price ranges to suit your customers' needs and budgets.

Keep in mind that "standard" doesn't mean "ordinary." Your baskets need to be stocked with items your customers won't find anywhere else. "Some of my things are on the expensive side, but they are unique," says Christine M. "You're never going to see one of my products in a supermarket or deli or wholesale club, and if you do, I'll cut the line and not use it anymore."

Custom baskets will often include items you purchase specifically for that basket. Most of these items will be bought at retail since you won't have had the advantage of buying in quantity, which means they'll be more expensive than your standard offerings. You'll need to explain this to your customers, find out beforehand how much they want to spend, and work within that budget. See the "Tracking Trends" checklist in Appendix C.

Know Thy Enemy

One of the most basic elements of effective marketing is differentiating your business from the competition. One marketing consultant calls it "eliminating the competition," because if you set yourself apart because no one else does exactly what you do, then you essentially have no competition. However, before you can differentiate yourself, you first need to understand who your competitors are and why your customers might buy from them. (See the "Market Research Survey" on page 31.)

There are two elements to competition: competing products and competing sources.

The primary products that compete with gift baskets are flowers and decorative indoor

> **Smart Tip**
>
> Put items people can readily use in your gift baskets. Though mixes—such as muffin mixes, bread mixes, even pasta flour—may look clever, most people don't want a gift that means they have to work.

plants. There is also a growing amount of competition from bouquet-style food items, such as fruit, cookies, and candy bouquets.

Gift baskets have a tremendous edge over such competing products because of their versatility and longevity. Certainly you could—and most likely will—include fresh or dried flowers, live plants, and food items in the baskets you make. In addition, you'll include a wide range of other gift and gourmet food items, and you can do it at comparable prices.

The sources that you'll be competing with include florists, gift shops, and, of late, warehouse stores.

Your primary competition will come from florists, since their products are quite similar to yours—flowers are delivered in baskets or vases and customized to each shopper's request and the recipient's special occasion—and their services include worldwide delivery and telephone orders. The best way to distinguish your service is to show how completely you can tailor a gift basket to the recipient's tastes and interests. You can also point out that your gift baskets don't need fresh water and won't fade in a matter of days. Depending on the contents of the basket, the gifts can last a long time. Also, while florists can arrange for deliveries in other cities, the company providing those flowers is not the one the customer is dealing with, and they lose a certain amount of quality control. You can create a basket your customer can see, then ship it anywhere in the world.

Competition will also come from greeting card, gift, and specialty stores, as well as gourmet candy, food, wine, and cigar shops. The advantage your service offers over these shops is that you assemble, wrap, and customize the gift for the giver, which saves them time. In addition, you offer one-stop shopping, combining numerous items into a single gift purchase they can present without having to run all over town.

Warehouse stores offer competitively priced gift baskets, and their selection increases substantially during holiday periods. However, those baskets are not personalized, and warehouse stores don't provide delivery.

As you conduct your market research, it's important to find out how your prospective customers' gift-buying needs are being met currently so you can develop a plan to convince them you will be a much better source.

Are You on a Mission?

At any given moment, most gift basket business owners have a very clear understanding of the mission of their company. They know what they are doing, how and where it's being done, and who their customers are. Problems can arise, however, when that mission is not clearly articulated into a statement, written down, and communicated to others.

Even in a very small company, a written mission statement helps everyone involved see the big picture and keeps them focused on the true goals of the business. At a minimum, your mission statement should define who your primary customers are; identify the products and services you produce; and describe the geographical location in which you operate. For example, your mission statement might read "Our mission is to provide businesses in the Toledo area with a resource for their gift-giving needs by designing, creating, and delivering high-quality custom gift baskets."

A mission statement should be short—usually just one sentence and certainly no more than two. A good idea is to cap it at 100 words. Anything longer than that isn't a mission statement and will probably confuse your employees. (To nail down your mission statement, fill out the worksheet on page 32.)

Once you've articulated your message, communicate it as often as possible to everyone in the company, along with customers and suppliers. Post it on the wall, hold meetings to talk about it, and include a reminder of the statement in other employee correspondence.

It's more important to adequately communicate the mission statement to employees than to customers. Sometimes companies try to use their mission statement for promotion, then as an aside use it to help their employees understand the business. That doesn't work very well. The most effective mission statements are developed strictly for internal communication and discussion, and then if something promotional comes out of it, great. In other words, your mission statement doesn't have to be clever or catchy—just accurate.

And although your mission statement may never win an advertising or creativity award, it can still be a very effective customer relations tool. One idea is to print your mission statement on a poster-sized panel, have every employee sign it, and hang it in a prominent place so customers can see it. You can even include it on your brochures and invoices.

Finally, make sure your suppliers know what your mission statement is; it will help them serve you better if they understand what you're all about.

Market Research Survey

Use the following questions to find out who your competition really is and what your prospective customers want. You can do telephone interviews with people and companies who fit the profile of your prospective customer. If you are considering a retail operation, spend some time outside the location and randomly ask passersby if they will answer a few questions. You can adjust the questions to suit your particular needs, so be sure you don't create a questionnaire so long and cumbersome that you annoy people with it. And although you can hand the questionnaire to people and ask them to fill it out and return it to you, you'll get better results if you ask the questions and record the answers yourself.

How many gift baskets do you typically buy? (A month, a quarter, a year) ____

_____

Are these for personal or business gifts? If both, what percentage are each?

_____

Do you buy custom or standard baskets? _____

Where are you currently buying your baskets? _____

_____

What do you especially like about that source? (Try to get two or three answers.)

_____

_____

_____

What is that source not doing that you would like them to do, or what could they be doing better? _____

_____

_____

What would a new gift basket company have to do to earn your business?

_____

_____

✔ Once your business is up and running, go back to the people you surveyed and let them know you're ready to meet their needs.

Mission Statement Worksheet

Fill in your mission statement on this worksheet. To develop an effective mission statement, ask yourself these questions:

○ Why does my company exist? Whom do we serve? What is our purpose?

○ What are our strengths, weaknesses, opportunities, and threats?

○ Considering the answers to the above questions, along with our expertise and resources, what business should we be in?

○ What is important to us? What do we stand for?

Mission Statement for

_____

(your business name)

_____

_____

_____

_____

_____

_____

4

Structuring
Your Business

There's a lot to do when you start a business. This chapter will address various issues you need to deal with as you get set up.

Naming Your Company

One of the most important marketing tools you will ever have is your company's name. A well-chosen name can work hard for you; an ineffective name means you have to work much harder at marketing your company.

Your company name should clearly identify what you do in a way that will appeal to your target market. It should be short, catchy, and memorable. It should also be easy to pronounce and spell—people who can't say your company name may use you themselves, but they won't refer you to anyone else. Look in Appendix B for a naming worksheet to help you choose the name for your company.

Bright Idea

When naming your company, consider creating a word that doesn't exist—that's what companies like Exxon and Kodak did. Just be sure the syllables blend to make an ear-appealing sound and that the name is simple enough for people to remember. Also, check to make sure you haven't inadvertently come up with a name that means something in another language.

One basketeer in Utah called her relatives across the country for help with naming her business. "I made them pull out their phone books and look up 'gift baskets.' There were very few at the time, so I also had them look up florists," S. Clift recalls. "As they would read me everybody's name, I would write down key words that I felt good about. I ended up with Your Best Impression because my company's goal was to make people aware that when I send out a gift basket, it's not from me; it's from them. To the person receiving it, it looks like the sender put a lot of thought and time into it, when they actually didn't."

Another gift basket business owner wanted a name that indicated she did more than just gift baskets—something like Baskets, et Cetera"—but most of the names she considered were already in use. The solution was to make up a name, so she coined Bask et Al, a name that would set her apart from the competition and accurately describe her company.

Still another basketeer says the name she chose for her company is her biggest regret. She took Baskets Frilled & Filled from a phrase she read in a magazine article, thinking at the time that it was a perfect description of what she was doing. But as her business evolves and she serves an increasing number of corporate accounts, she thinks the name is too "froufrou" for her market. Also, although the store name is indeed memorable, she often has to repeat it several times and even spell it for people to understand it.

Though naming your company is without a doubt a creative process, it helps to take a systematic approach. Once you've decided on a name, or perhaps two or three possibilities, take the following steps:

- *Check the name for effectiveness and functionality.* Does it quickly and easily convey what you do? Is it easy to say and spell? Don't just imagine answering the phone with it; pick up the phone and try it a few times. Is it memorable in a positive way? Ask several of your friends and associates to serve as a focus group to help you evaluate the name's impact.

- *Search for potential conflicts in your local market.* Find out if any other local or regional business serving your market area—whether it has to do with gift baskets or not—has a name so similar that yours might confuse the public.

- *Check for legal availability.* Exactly how you do this depends on the legal structure you choose. Typically, sole proprietorships and partnerships operating under a name other than that of the owner(s) are required by the county, city, or state to register their fictitious name. Even if it's not required, it's a good idea, because that means no one else can use that name. To find out how to register a fictitious name in your state, start by calling the local business licensing agency; for example, in New Hampshire you do that with the secretary of state. They'll either be able to tell you or can refer you to the correct agency. Corporations usually operate under their corporate name. In either case, you need to check with the appropriate regulatory agency to be sure the name you choose is available.

- *Check for use on the internet.* If someone else is already using your name as a domain site on the World Wide Web, consider coming up with something else—the use could be confusing to your customers. And besides, in this business age you should be planning to create your own website.

- *Check to see if the name conflicts with any name listed on your state's trademark register.* Your state's department of commerce can help you or direct you to the correct agency. You should also check with the trademark register maintained by the U.S. Patent and Trademark Office (PTO). Visit their website at uspto.gov.

Once the name you've chosen passes these tests, you need to protect it by registering it with the appropriate state agency; again, your state's department of commerce can help you. If you expect to be doing business on a national level—for example, if you'll be handling mail orders or operating on the web—you should also register the name with the PTO.

> **Bright Idea**
>
> Once you've narrowed down your name search to three or four choices, test-market your ideas by asking a small group of people who fit the profile of your potential customer what they think of the names you're considering. Find out what kind of company the name makes them think of and if they'd feel comfortable buying gift baskets from a company with that name. Finally, get them to explain the reasoning behind their answers.

Trademarks

Trademark issues go beyond the name of your company to include the names of the products you'll create and even the names of the items you'll be including in your baskets. What exactly is a trademark? According to the PTO, "A trademark includes any word, name, symbol, or device, or any combination, used or intended to be used in commerce to identify and distinguish the goods of one manufacturer or seller from goods manufactured or sold by others, and to indicate the source of the goods. In short, a trademark is a brand name."

In addition to your company name, if you spend a lot of time coming up with unusual names for your line of gift baskets, you may want to trademark them to keep anyone else from using them. This is not a common practice in the industry, and to qualify to be trademarked, the name must be truly unique—"Baby Basket" or "Birthday Cheer" are not examples of unique names. If in the course of growing your business, you develop other unique products, such as special gift or food items, you may want to consider trademarking the names and patenting the products.

Registering your trademark is not essential, but it does offer some benefits. It gives notice to the public of your claim of ownership of the mark, a legal presumption of ownership nationwide, and the exclusive right to use the mark on or in connection with the goods or services set forth in the registration.

You can access information about the process of applying for trademark protection and patents on the web or by contacting the PTO by phone.

On the Mark

Just as you don't want anyone infringing on your trademark, so should you not infringe on others'.

You may want to use trademarks in your brochures or marketing materials when describing the contents of your baskets. This is most commonly done with gourmet food items such as specialty coffees and gourmet chocolates. The fact that you use products with easily recognizable and respected names will enhance your own marketing efforts, and your customers will appreciate knowing exactly what is going into the baskets they're buying.

Using another company's product name under these circumstances is quite common and most manufacturers will cooperate with you. Just be sure you check with them so that the issue is handled in a way that meets with their approval.

Protect Your Mark

Once you've established a trademark, you must use it or you risk losing it. Trademarks not actively used for two or more years may be considered abandoned—which means someone else can begin using the mark and you will have no recourse.

You also need to control your mark. Do not allow others to use your mark without your consent or without restricting what product or service it represents. Think about how companies like McDonald's and Walt Disney aggressively pursue unauthorized use of their trademarks. They understand how much they have to lose if they fail to control their marks.

If you discover someone using your mark without your authorization, consult with an attorney to determine the most appropriate and effective action.

Legal Structure

One of the first decisions you'll need to make about your new gift basket business is the legal structure of your company. This is an important decision that can affect your financial liability, the amount of taxes you pay, the degree of ultimate control you have over the company, as well as your ability to raise money, attract investors, and ultimately sell the business. However, legal structure shouldn't be confused with operating structure. Attorney Robert S. Bernstein, a managing partner with the Bernstein Law Firm P.C. in Pittsburgh, explains the difference: "The legal structure is the ownership structure—who actually owns the company. The operating structure defines who makes management decisions and runs the company."

A sole proprietorship is owned by the proprietor; a partnership is owned by the partners; and a corporation is owned by the shareholders. Sole proprietorships and partnerships can be operated however the owners choose. In a corporation, typically, the shareholders elect directors, who in turn elect officers, who then employ other people to run and work in the company. But it's entirely possible for a corporation to have only one shareholder and to essentially function as a sole proprietorship. In any case, how you plan to operate the company should not be a major factor in your choice of legal structures.

So what goes into choosing a legal structure? The first point to consider, says Bernstein, is who is actually making the decision on the legal structure. If you're starting the company by yourself, you don't need to take anyone else's preferences into consideration. "But if there are multiple people involved, you need to consider how you're going to relate to each other in the business," he says. "You also need to consider the issue of asset protection and limiting your liability in the event things don't go well."

Something else to think about is your target customers and what their perception will be of your structure. While it's not necessarily true, says Bernstein, "there is a tendency to believe that the legal form of a business has some relationship to the sophistication of the owners, with the sole proprietor as the least and the corporation as the most sophisticated." If your target market is going to be other businesses, it might enhance your image if you incorporate.

Your image notwithstanding, the biggest advantage of forming a corporation is in the area of asset protection, which, says Bernstein, is the process of making sure the assets you don't want to put into the business don't stand liable for the business debt. However, to take advantage of the protection a corporation offers, you must respect the corporation's identity. That means maintaining the corporation as a separate entity; keeping your corporate and personal funds separate, even if you are the sole shareholder; and following your state's rules regarding the holding of annual meetings and other record-keeping requirements.

Is any one of these structures better than another? No. We found basketeers operating as sole proprietors, partners, and corporations, and they made their choices based on what was best for their particular situation. Choose the form that is most appropriate for your particular needs.

Do you need an attorney to set it up? Again, no. Bernstein says there are plenty of good do-it-yourself books and kits on the market, and most of the state agencies that oversee corporations have guidelines you can use. Even so, it's always a good idea to have a lawyer at least look over your documents before you file them, just to make sure they are complete and will allow you to truly function as you want.

Finally, remember that your choice of legal structure is not an irrevocable decision, although if you're going to make a switch, it's easier to go from the simpler forms to the more sophisticated ones than the other way around. Bernstein says the typical pattern is to start as a sole proprietor, then move up to a corporation as the business grows. But if you need the asset protection of a corporation from the beginning, start out that way. "If you're going to the trouble to start a business, decide on a structure, and put it all together, it's worth the extra effort to make sure it's really going to work," says Bernstein.

Licenses and Permits

Most cities and counties require business operators to obtain various licenses and permits to comply with local regulations. While you're still in the planning stages, check with your local planning and zoning department or city/county business license department to find out what licenses and permits you will need and what is involved in obtaining them. You may need some or all of the following:

- *Occupational license or permit.* This is typically required by the city (or county if you are not within an incorporated city) for just about every business operating within its jurisdiction. License fees are essentially a tax, and the rates vary widely, based on the location and type of business. As part of the application process, the licensing bureau will check to make sure there are no zoning restrictions prohibiting you from operating.

- *Health department permit.* If you are going to include food items in your gift baskets, you may need a permit from your local health department. Requirements may vary depending on whether you are actually preparing and packaging the food yourself or purchasing packaged food from other vendors, which you then include in your baskets. An inspector will visit your facility before issuing the permit.

- *Beer, wine, and liquor licenses.* To sell alcoholic beverages, you need to be licensed by your state and generally must operate from a commercial rather than a homebased location. Liquor licensing laws vary widely by state. Most gift basket business owners avoid this issue by refusing to sell alcoholic beverages. If a customer wants a bottle of wine, champagne, or liquor in a basket, explain that they must purchase the alcohol elsewhere and bring it to you so you can include it in the basket.

- *Fire department permit.* If you use any flammable materials or if your business is open to the public, you may be required to have a permit from the local fire department.

- *Sign permit.* Many cities and suburbs have sign ordinances that restrict the size, location, and sometimes the lighting and type of sign you can use in front of your business. Landlords may also impose their own restrictions. Most residential areas forbid signs altogether. To avoid costly mistakes, check regulations and secure the written approval of your landlord before you invest in a sign.

- *State licenses.* Many states require persons engaged in certain occupations to hold licenses or occupational permits. Often, these people must pass state examinations before they can conduct business. States commonly require licensing for auto mechanics, plumbers, electricians, building contractors, collection agents, insurance agents, real estate brokers, repossessors, and personal service providers such as doctors, nurses, barbers, cosmetologists, etc. It is highly unlikely that you will need a state license to operate your gift basket business, but it's a good idea to check with your state's occupation licensing entity to be sure.

> **Beware!**
> Find out what type of licenses and permits are required for your business while you're still in the planning stage. You may find out you can't legally operate the business you're envisioning, so give yourself time to make adjustments to your strategy before you've spent a lot of time and money trying to move in an impossible direction.

Business Insurance

It takes a lot to start a business, even a small one, so protect your investment with adequate insurance. If you're homebased, don't assume your homeowner's or renter's policy covers your business equipment; chances are, it doesn't. If you're located in a commercial facility, be prepared for your landlord to require proof of certain levels of liability insurance when you sign the lease. And in either case, you need coverage for your inventory and other valuables.

A smart approach to insurance is to find an agent who works with businesses similar to yours. The agent should be willing to help you analyze your needs, evaluate what risks you're willing to accept and what risks you need to insure against, and work with you to keep your insurance costs down.

> **Tip...**
>
> **Smart Tip**
>
> When you purchase insurance on your equipment and inventory, ask what documentation the insurance company requires before you ever have to file a claim. That way, you'll be sure to maintain appropriate records, and the claims process will be easier if it is ever necessary.

Typically, homebased gift basket business owners will want to make sure their equipment and inventory are covered against theft, fire, flood, and other perils, and that they have some liability protection if someone (either a customer or an employee) is injured on their property or by their product. In most cases, one of the new insurance policies designed for homebased businesses will provide sufficient coverage. Also, if you use your vehicle for business, be sure it is appropriately covered.

> **Tip...**
>
> **Smart Tip**
>
> Sit down with your insurance agent on an annual basis and review your insurance needs. As your company grows, it's sure to change. Also, insurance companies are always developing new products to meet the needs of the growing small-business market, and it's possible that one of these new policies will be more appropriate for you.

If you opt for a commercial location, you'll find your landlord will probably require certain levels of general liability coverage as part of the terms of your lease. You'll also want to cover your inventory, equipment, and fixtures. Once your business is up and running, consider business interruption insurance to replace lost revenue and cover related costs if you are ever unable to operate due to covered circumstances.

Although you can fall into the "insurance poor" trap, there are lots of insurances to consider. Review the "Insurance Planning Worksheet" in Appendix C.

Professional Services

As a business owner, you may be the boss, but you can't be expected to know everything. You'll occasionally need to turn to professionals for information and assistance. It's a good idea to identify and establish a relationship with these professionals before you get into a crisis situation.

To shop for a professional service provider, ask friends and associates for recommendations. You might also check with your local chamber of commerce or trade association for referrals. Find someone who understands your industry and specific business and appears eager to work with you. Check them out with the Better Business Bureau and the appropriate state licensing agency before committing yourself.

As a gift basket business owner, the professional service providers you're likely to need include:

- *Attorney.* You need a lawyer who understands and practices in the area of business law, is honest, and appreciates your patronage. In most parts of the United States, there are an abundance of lawyers willing to compete fiercely for the privilege of serving you. Interview several, and choose one you feel comfortable with. Be sure to clarify the fee schedule ahead of time, and get your agreement in writing. Keep in mind that good commercial lawyers don't come cheap; if you want good advice, you must be willing to pay for it. Your attorney should review all contracts, leases, letters of intent, and other legal documents before you sign them. They can also help you with collecting bad debts and establishing personnel policies and procedures. Of course, if you are unsure of the legal ramifications of any situation, call your attorney immediately.

- *Accountant.* Among your outside advisors, your accountant is likely to have the greatest impact on the success or failure of your business. If you are forming a corporation, your accountant should counsel you on tax issues during the startup. On an ongoing basis, your accountant can help you organize the statistical data concerning your business, assist in charting future actions based on past performance, and advise you on your overall financial strategy regarding purchasing, capital investment, and other matters related to your business goals. A good accountant will also serve as a tax advisor, making sure you are in compliance with all applicable regulations and don't overpay any taxes.

- *Insurance agent.* A good independent insurance agent can assist you with all aspects of your business insurance, from general liability to employee benefits, and can probably even handle your personal insurance as well. Look for an agent who works with a wide range of insurers and understands your particular business. This agent should be willing to explain the details of various types of coverage, consult with you to determine the most appropriate coverage, help

Accountant Interview

Just because the person you are hiring is a professional, don't think they are in the driver's seat. They need your business as much, if not more, than you need theirs. Finding the right professionals for your business and your personality is a fine art. Plan to interview the professionals you sign on with—after all, you want them with you for the life of your company.

For instance, if you are looking for an accountant, ask the following questions:

❍ Are you a Certified Public Accountant?

❍ Are you licensed to practice in this state? (Don't assume anything!)

❍ Where did you graduate from? (Don't just ask if she went to school; she could have dropped out after two semesters and still not lie answering this question affirmatively.)

❍ Who are some of your clients? (Be sure to give them a quick call and ask how they feel about doing business with this accountant.)

❍ What is your area of specialization? (You want this answer to be "retail" or at least "small businesses." If you are homebased, it would be best if the accountant had expertise in homebased businesses.)

❍ What is the size of the majority of your clients? (Someone who has mostly huger corporate clients probably isn't going to be the right match for a small retail gift basket business.)

❍ When can I contact you? (You want a sense of how accessible the accountant will be to you.)

❍ What are your fees? (Make sure you know upfront how much the accountant's services are going to cost you.)

you understand the degree of risk you are taking, work with you in developing risk-reduction programs, and assist in expediting any claims.

- *Banker.* You need a business bank account and a relationship with a banker. Don't just choose the bank you've always done your personal banking with; it may not be the best bank for your business. Interview several bankers before making a decision on where to place your business. Once your account is opened, maintain a relationship with the banker. Periodically sit down and review your accounts and the services you use to make sure you are getting the package most appropriate for your situation. Ask for advice if you're having financial questions or problems. When the time comes that you need a loan, or a bank reference to provide to creditors, the relationship you've established will work in your favor.

- *Consultants.* The consulting industry is booming, and for good reason. Consultants can provide valuable, objective input on all aspects of your business. Consider hiring a business consultant to evaluate your business plan or a marketing consultant to assist you in that area. When you are ready to hire employees, a human resources consultant may help you avoid some costly mistakes. Consulting fees vary widely, depending on the individual's experience, location, and field of expertise. If you can't afford to hire a consultant, consider contacting the business school at the nearest college or university and hiring an MBA student to help you.

- *Computer expert.* If you don't know much about computers, find someone to help you select a system and the appropriate software, and who will be available to help you maintain, troubleshoot, and expand your system as you need it. If you're going to pursue internet sales, use a professional web page designer to set up and maintain your site. Just as you wouldn't send out an amateurish basket, you shouldn't put up an unprofessional web page.

Create Your Own Advisory Board

Not even the president of the United States is expected to know everything. That's why he surrounds himself with advisors—experts in particular areas who provide

The Hidden Profit Eater

Freight is a variable expense that can be hard to predict but has a definite—and often significant—impact on your bottom line. As you shop for and build relationships with suppliers, consider where they are located and how much it will cost for you to receive their goods.

Track your freight costs carefully, and be sure each charge is accurate. It's a good idea to periodically check to make sure the weight of the shipment matches the weight you were charged for. And if your supplier prepays the freight charges and adds it to your merchandise invoice, verify that the rates have been correctly calculated.

If you buy primarily from local suppliers and pick up the merchandise yourself, you still need to consider the cost of getting the material from their location to yours. In this situation, your time and vehicle expenses need to be considered as "freight costs" when calculating a fair and reasonable markup for the goods.

knowledge and information to help him make decisions. Savvy small-business owners use a similar strategy.

You can assemble a team of volunteer advisors to meet with you periodically to offer advice and direction. Because this isn't an official or legal entity, you have a great deal of latitude in how you set it up. Advisory boards can be structured to help both with the direct operation of your company as well as the task of keeping you informed on various business, legal, and financial trends that may affect you. Use these tips to set up your board:

- *Structure a board that meets your needs.* Generally, you'll want a legal advisor, an accountant, a marketing expert, a human resources person, and perhaps a financial advisor. You may also want successful entrepreneurs from other industries who understand the basics of business and will view your operation with a fresh eye.

- *Ask the most successful people you can find, even if you don't know them well.* You'll be surprised at how willing people are to help another business succeed.

- *Be clear about what you are trying to do.* Let your prospective advisors know what your goals are and that you don't expect them to take on an active management role or to assume any liability for your company or for the advice they offer.

- *Don't worry about compensation.* Advisory board members are rarely compensated with more than lunch or dinner. Of course, if a member of your board provides a direct service—for example, if an attorney reviews a contract or an accountant prepares a financial statement—then they should be paid at their normal rate. But that's not part of their job as an advisory board member. Keep in mind that, even though you don't write them a check, your advisory board members will likely benefit in a variety of tangible and nontangible ways. Being on your board will expose them to ideas and perspectives they may not otherwise see and will also expand their own network.

- *Consider the group dynamics when holding meetings.* You may want to meet with all the members together or in small groups of one or two. It all depends on how they relate to each other and what you need to accomplish.

- *Ask for honesty, and don't be offended when you get it.* Your pride might be hurt when someone points out something you are doing wrong, but the awareness will be beneficial in the long run.

- *Learn from failure as well as success.* Encourage board members to tell you about their mistakes so you can avoid repeating them.

- *Respect the contribution your board members are making.* Let them know you appreciate how busy they are, and don't abuse or waste their time.

- *Make it fun.* You are, after all, asking these people to donate their time, so create a pleasant atmosphere. Snacks at meetings are always welcome.

- *Listen to every piece of advice.* Stop talking and listen. You don't have to follow every piece of advice, but you need to hear it.

- *Provide feedback to the board.* Good or bad, let the board know what you did and what the results were.

Shipping and Receiving

Most gift basket businesses have to deal with shipping and receiving on a regular basis, both to send baskets out and to receive inventory and supplies. A lot of how much you use shipping services will depend on the way your business is set up. Even if you have a retail location, don't underestimate how important shipping will be; the number of customers walking in the door to order a basket and walking out with the basket in hand will probably be a fraction of the amount of business that requires shipping. Local customers who call or come in to order a basket will most likely still want the basket shipped to the recipient.

If your basket business is mostly catalog- or web-based, shipping will be key to the success of your business. It will be beneficial to your bottom line to do lots of research and come up with the best way to ship your orders. And you may find you choose a different carrier for different types of baskets.

Most of your shipments will be small enough to be handled by carriers like United Parcel Service (UPS). Contact their customer service department to set up an account so they can bill you and to arrange for daily pickups if you need them.

All of the major carriers are pretty aggressively targeting business package mailers; Federal Express, known mainly as an express carrier, started their "ground service" offering three- to five-day delivery. And of course there is always the U.S. Postal Service. Contact your local post office to find out what they have to offer.

Dollar Stretcher

When it comes to freight services, don't pay for more than you need. Most overnight companies offer two or three levels of next-day service—early morning, before noon, and afternoon. The earlier the guaranteed delivery, the higher the cost. If next afternoon will meet your customer's needs, don't pay for morning delivery. And if the carrier misses their delivery commitment, insist that they honor their guarantee by refunding the charges.

Don't be afraid to ask for quantity discounts! If you do a lot of business with one company, you can expect to get lower rates. Again, take the time to do lots of homework to find what works the best for your type of business.

Don't overlook the idea of local delivery services and regional freight carriers. Many of these carriers offer competitive rates and are hungry for your business.

Shop around for the best price/service package.

Freight is an important part of your business, from both a price and service standpoint. The cost of freight is a direct expense that affects your bottom line and needs to be calculated into your pricing. And when the freight company makes a mistake, is late with a delivery, or loses or damages a package, it could have a seriously negative impact on your relationship with your customers. So choose your freight companies carefully, and demand that they perform up to your high standards.

Shipping Supplies

Choosing packaging to ship your baskets can be an art in itself. Shop around; there are myriad styles of cartons available to cover whatever you need. You will want to make sure the carton is sturdy enough to protect its contents but not so heavy that it adds greatly to the shipping costs.

If you have a line of standard baskets for sale, you will find that you can order cartons in large quantities that are perfect for that line, and you will save money in the process. Custom orders will probably require custom packaging. Shop around in advance to know where you can make last-minute purchases for what you need, or look online in case you have time to have something sent overnight.

Beware!

Never just sign a delivery receipt for packages. Even though you'll get to know your regular driver, always count the packages and do a quick visual inspection for external signs of damage.

Incoming

Another important aspect of shipping is the supplies you receive. Keep on top of your receiving shipping costs. Take advantage of specials that offer free shipping where you can, but don't buy more of something than you need just because they are offering free shipping—if you do the math, you probably will be spending more in the long run for supplies you will never use. Companies often offer free shipping as a trade show special, so if you go to any of the gift shows look for those offers. And if you are about to order from a company, check to see if they are going to have a free shipping offer at the show. If you can wait, hold your order until the show; if you can't wait, don't be afraid to ask if you can get the show special in advance.

Finances
Keep the
Cash Flowing

In business, there are two key sides to the issue
of money: how much you need to start and operate, and how
much you can expect to take in. Analyzing these numbers is often
extremely difficult for small-business owners who typically would
rather be in the trenches getting the work done than bound to a
desk dealing with tiresome numbers.

However, dealing with the numbers on some level is critical. No business stays in business without a good handle on revenue and expenses. You as the owner don't have to be the one taking care of the details of keeping the books—Gift Baskets by Your Design owner Dana S. advises to definitely "Spend money for someone to do your books." But you as the owner should have some sort of handle on how much revenue you are generating, how much you are spending in expenses, and how much things cost, as well as having a pretty solid finger on your budget for purchasing, hiring, etc.

But before you get into looking back on revenue and expenses, it's important to look forward before you spend a dime. You do that with something called a business plan.

Creating a Business Plan

You may think that since you plan to start a relatively low-key business you don't need to go to the time and effort needed to create a business plan. And you would be wrong. A business plan provides you with many advantages:

- It is a great way to think through the details of your business.
- It is almost a must if you plan to get any outside funding.
- It provides a road map for your business that you can look back on when you feel things are getting a little lost.
- It is a great guide for expanding your business down the road.

Books and websites with sample business plans abound, and you should look at a few before you dig into your own. Don't be intimidated thinking you can't pull this together. If you aren't "a writer," find a friend or freelance writer who can help you; if you aren't "good at math," look for an accountant who will help you pull together the appropriate financials. It is definitely worth it.

Besides books and websites with general information, there are also many business plan templates available to make it easy to plug in your information. The templates will guide you to cover the things that are expected out of a business plan. Also, look to resources like the Small Business Administration and the retired executive program SCORE. They will have lots of useful information on this important part of your business's development.

Whatever route you take, consider the business plan your key to understanding every nook and cranny of your business. The following outlines the main areas your business plan should cover. (See Appendix C for the "Business Plan Checklist.")

An Overview

A business plan should start with a general overview of the business you plan to start. Talk about the gift basket business you envision and why you chose this business type. Be excited about it without being too goofy! Talk about the niche you plan to fill. The overview should ground the reader enough to make the rest of the business plan make sense.

Business Logistics

Where do you plan to locate your business? Will it be a retail gift basket shop or is it going to be strictly via catalogs and a website? What kind warehousing do you need and where will that be? This is where the reader gets a sense of the specific business you are opening.

Market and Marketing

You need to explain how you determined there is a market for a gift basket business in the area you are setting up shop in. If you are not creating a retail location, what were the factors that led you to determine that there is room for another mailorder gift basket business? What customer type do you plan to target and how do you know they spend money on gift baskets? That's all your market.

As for market-*ing*, this is where you tell how you are going to let those potential customers know you exist. And when you announce yourself to them, how are you going to entice them to buy your gift baskets? This is where you talk about how the gift basket industry tends to operate—will you use newspaper ads, radio, e-newsletters, coupons?

Your Background

Spend a couple paragraphs talking about your background. How have you prepared to become an entrepreneur? What will make you good at running a gift basket business?

If you plan to have partners, what are their credentials? And what exactly will they do within the business?

If you plan to hire employees early on, tell who those employees will be (two part-time cashiers and one gift basket designer, for example) and what they will do to help bring in business.

Business Structure

This brief section can cover what kind of business structure you have chosen for your business—a sole proprietorship where you and the business are essentially one and the same thing and the business's income is reported to the IRS as personal income? Or a type of corporation with a separate identity? Or a partnership? And talk briefly about how/when that might change in the future.

The Numbers

Numbers need to be crunched even before you take your first order! You will want to do monthly revenue projections for the first year of business. These projections are determined by how much revenue should be generated by certain sales tools, like the mailing of a catalog or eight corporate presentations per month, or however you plan to focus your sales efforts.

Another spreadsheet you will need is a detailed breakdown of one year of expenses—the costs of the items you put in the baskets sold in that period, advertising expenses, employee salaries if applicable, etc. And then you will need to do a balance sheet where you deduct the expenses from the revenue for each month for a one-year period and see where you stand.

Dollar Stretcher

Create your own informal buying co-op with one or two other gift basket businesses. Many of the major suppliers won't accept small orders or give substantial quantity discounts to small accounts. Teaming up with another company to increase the size of your order can mean significant savings, and can also open doors to suppliers you might not otherwise be able to buy from.

How much more financial detail you need depends on what you plan to do with your business plan. If you intend to use it to seek financing from a bank, you will want as much financial detail as possible. If you aren't numbers-savvy, it will pay to have an accountant put these spreadsheets together for you; banks are very impressed by realistic detailed financials.

If your business plan will be used mainly to guide you in the growth of your business, then you can decide how much financial detail you want to estimate upfront.

This is all a lot of work to put together, no question. But it is definitely worth it even for no other reason than to clarify your business framework in your mind and guide you as you proceed from a great idea to opening your doors.

SWOT Analysis

In considering your overall business idea, a common business tool to use is the SWOT Analysis. SWOT stands for Strengths, Weaknesses, Opportunities, and Threats. These categories cover the following:

- *Strengths:* Things that make your business different from your competitors' businesses. This includes you and your personal experience.
- *Weaknesses:* Things you will need to work on to get up to snuff for your business and that your competitors could take advantage of until you overcome these weaknesses.

▲

Sample SWOT Analysis

Strengths

○ My ten years of experience in the gift industry.

○ My excellent communications skills.

○ My hobby crafting skills.

Weaknesses

○ My lack of computer expertise.

○ The need to make this a homebased business to be home with my children.

Opportunities

○ My connections in the gift industry that can help me find product at high discount.

○ The gift basket industry can thrive on a specialized niche that isn't being served.

Threats

○ The economy is in a downturn and gifts can be the first to be cut from individuals or corporate budgets.

○ The zoning laws in my town are s in the process of being rewritten and homebased businesses may have stricter regulations.

- *Opportunities:* What might benefit your company at this moment in time?
- *Threats:* What do your competitors have that you don't? What other things can harm the success of your business?

Brainstorm at least a couple things in each category that apply to your idea. Above is a sample SWOT Analysis that might be for a gift basket business. Use a form like this if you are starting a new business, a new idea for your existing business, or if you are purchasing a business. It can be included in your business plan to show your potential lenders that you have thought your business through thoroughly.

Sources of Startup Funds

Most of the basketeers we spoke with used personal savings to start their businesses. Traditional financing is difficult to obtain, especially for homebased businesses—but you have plenty of other ways to raise money to get started. Some suggestions:

- *Your own resources.* Do a thorough inventory of your assets. People generally have more assets than they immediately realize. This could include savings accounts, equity in real estate, retirement accounts, vehicles, recreation equipment, collections, and other investments. You may opt to sell assets for cash or use them as collateral for a loan. Also take a look at your personal line of credit. Many successful businesses have been started with credit cards.

- *Friends and family.* The next logical step after gathering your own resources is to approach friends and relatives who believe in you and want to help you succeed. Be cautious with these arrangements; no matter how close you are, present yourself professionally, put everything in writing, and be sure the individuals you approach can afford to take the risk of investing in your business.

- *Partners.* Using the "strength in numbers" principle, look around for someone who may want to team up with you in your venture. You may choose someone who has financial resources and wants to work side by side with you in the business. Or you may find someone who has money to invest but no interest in doing the actual work. Be sure to create a written partnership agreement that clearly defines your respective responsibilities and obligations.

- *Government programs.* Take advantage of the abundance of local, state, and federal programs designed to support small businesses. Make your first stop the U.S. Small Business Administration, then investigate various other programs.

> **Bright Idea**
>
> If you are turning your hobby into a business, be sure to let everyone you've ever given a basket to in the past know that they can now purchase your creations to give to their own friends and associates.

Women, minorities, and veterans should check out niche financing possibilities designed to help these groups get into business. The business section of your local library is a good place to begin your research.

How Much Do You Need?

One basketeer we talked with started her business with $300 cash; another plunged $25,000 into her new company before ever opening the doors. Both companies are profitable today.

Calculate how much you need to start your ideal business, then figure out how much you have. If you have all the cash you need, you're very fortunate. If you don't, you need to start playing with the numbers and deciding what you can do without.

The checklist on page 57 will serve as a guide for creating a startup budget for your gift basket business. Prices for supplies and equipment are estimated ranges and will vary depending on features, sources, and whether they are new or used. Price ranges beginning with $0 are either optional or items you are already likely to own and therefore don't need to purchase.

Don't forget to also factor in rent (unless you're homebased), business license, utility deposits, insurance, any legal and accounting services, and your grand opening advertising.

Use the worksheet on page 59 to pencil in and then tally up all your costs. If you copy a couple of extra sheets first, you can compare various options, decide which will work the best for you, and then arrive at your "Official Startup Figure."

Appendix D contains several financial worksheets to help you with the financial side of your business and business plan.

SBA Loans

The SBA offers numerous loan programs to assist small businesses. The SBA does not actually lend the money; it is primarily a guarantor of loans made by private institutions. Their website offers the following list of the types of financial assistance offered by the SBA that might be of interest to someone starting up a gift basket business:

PROGRAM: Basic 7(a) Loan Guarantee

FUNCTION: Serves as the SBA's primary business loan program to help qualified small businesses obtain financing when they might not be eligible for business loans through normal lending channels. Loan proceeds can be used for most sound business purposes including working capital, machinery and equipment, furniture and fixtures, land and building (including purchase, renovation, and new construction), leasehold improvements, and debt refinancing (under special conditions). Loan maturity is up to 10 years for working capital and generally up to 25 years for fixed assets.

CUSTOMER: Startup and existing small businesses, commercial lending institutions.

DELIVERED THROUGH: Commercial lending institutions.

PROGRAM: Microloan, a 7(m) Loan Program

FUNCTION: Provides short-term loans of up to $35,000 to small businesses and not-for-profit child-care centers for working capital or the purchase of inventory, supplies, furniture, fixtures, machinery, and/or equipment.

▲

SBA Loans, continued

Proceeds cannot be used to pay existing debts or to purchase real estate. The SBA makes or guarantees a loan to an intermediary, who in turn, makes the microloan to the applicant. These organizations also provide management and technical assistance. The loans are not guaranteed by the SBA. The microloan program is available in selected locations in most states.

CUSTOMER: Small businesses and not-for-profit child-care centers needing small-scale financing and technical assistance for startup or expansion.

DELIVERED THROUGH: Specially designated intermediary lenders (nonprofit organizations with experience in lending and in technical assistance).

PROGRAM: Loan Prequalification

FUNCTION: Allows business applicants to have their loan applications for $250,000 or less analyzed and potentially sanctioned by the SBA before they are taken to lenders for consideration. The program focuses on the applicant's character, credit, experience, and reliability rather than assets. An SBA-designated intermediary works with the business owner to review and strengthen the loan application. The review is based on key financial ratios, credit and business history, and the loan-request terms. The program is administered by the SBA's Office of Field Operations and SBA district offices.

CUSTOMER: Designated small businesses.

DELIVERED THROUGH: Intermediaries operating in specific geographic areas.

To learn about other SBA loan programs, and about other services offered by the SBA, check their comprehensive website at sba.gov.

Turning Pro

Most of the basketeers we interviewed had made at least some gift baskets just for fun before starting their businesses, and they all knew of other operators who started out as hobbyists. One of the biggest pitfalls of taking this route to business ownership is failing to make the complete transition from amateur to professional.

One basketeer says the two most common mistakes she sees from new gift basket business owners is not making a complete and serious commitment to customer service, and pricing too low because what you're doing is "fun."

No matter how much pleasure you derive from creating gift baskets, this is a product your customers are paying money for, and you must respect the fact that this is a business transaction. And although it's tempting to undercut prices both to get new business and because you enjoy making baskets so much that you'd do it whether you got paid or not, that's simply a bad business strategy. It will hurt your business individually, and the industry collectively, because you make it more difficult for others to charge fair prices—even long after you have given up because you didn't make any money.

Stat Fact
According to the latest survey by *Gift Basket Review* magazine, the average price of a consumer gift basket is now at $48.41. The average price of a corporate gift basket is at $61.89.

If you have been making gift baskets as a hobby and have decided to turn that hobby into a profitable business, you need to take yourself seriously and run your company like the professional operation you want it to be.

One of the most important issues you'll have to deal with is record keeping. "When you want to buy something for your hobby, you just do it—it doesn't matter if you pay with cash or credit card, or if you keep the receipt," says CPA Vicki Helmick. "But in business, those details are critical."

The Price Is Right

Pricing can be tedious and time-consuming, especially if you don't have a knack for juggling numbers. If your prices are too low, you rob yourself of profits or are forced to reduce the quality of your product to maintain your profitability. If your prices are too high, you may lose business.

Theoretically, you should price every item you carry to cover its wholesale cost, labor costs, freight charges, a proportionate share of your overhead, and a reasonable profit. In reality, some items will warrant a high gross profit and others will require a low or no gross profit for you to move them quickly. Also, calculating overhead costs, such as unpredictable insurance rates, shrinkage (shoplifting, employee or other theft, shippers' mistakes), and other unexpected expenses can add to the challenge of pricing. As long as the aggregate gross and net profits are sufficiently high, your business will be successful.

Most gift basket business operators expect to net 15 percent to 30 percent of their gross revenue, and they typically reach this goal by applying a 100 percent markup to the cost of the items in the basket.

▲

Whether you are turning your hobby into a business or simply starting a business because this is what you want to do, Helmick offers these suggestions:

- *Open a separate checking account for the business.* Your bank account balance is a quick and easy way to see how well you're doing, but you won't have a clear picture unless you're using an account that is strictly for business income and expenses.

- *Get a credit card for the business.* You may not be able to get the card in the business name, but at least have one card that is used exclusively for business expenses. This helps you keep your records in order and—if the card is in the business name—helps you establish business credit.

- *Invest in a retirement plan.* Beyond the long-term benefits, a retirement plan offers some short-term advantages. You will not only reduce your current taxes, but if you are a homebased sole proprietor, the fact that you show a retirement plan on your income tax return indicates to the IRS that you are serious about your business, not just trying to take some questionable deductions.

- *Document your equipment.* If you purchased basket-making equipment as part of your hobby and can prove the cost involved, you may be able to deduct those expenses on your tax return after you've formed your company. Talk to your tax advisor for specifics on how to do this.

- *Figure out how much it actually costs you to put together a basket.* Besides the cost of the merchandise, calculate overhead, your time, freight, special handling, and any other expenses. Be especially careful about tracking your time; too many business owners fail to give their time the value it deserves.

> ### Smart Tip
> *Tip...*
>
> Basketeers often short-change themselves on labor when setting prices. Be sure you know how long it really takes you to assemble, package, and deliver or ship a basket; put together several of varying complexity, and time yourself—don't estimate. Then figure out how much you want to earn for your labor, and add that to the cost of the basket.

Estimated Startup Expenses

Item	Price
Specialty Equipment	
Work space fixtures	$500–$2,000
Work table(s)	$80–$400
Crafting tools	$50–$150
Shrink wrapper	$300–$500
Heat gun	$50–$80
Company vehicle	$0–$7,000
Signage	$0–$1,400
Security system	$0–$2,500
Storage Fixtures and Hardware	
Storage shelves, cabinets	$100–$500
Store Equipment/Fixtures (for retail operations)	
Special displays and related hardware	$0–$1,000
Display shelving	$0–$800
Cash register	$0–$500
Counter	$0–$750
Marking guns (1 or 2)	$0–$85
Floor gondolas (5 to 10)	$0–$4,000
Pegboard (5 to 10 panels)	$0–$550
Hooks	$0–$110
Showcases (1 or 2)	$0–$800
Wall gondolas (5 to 10)	$0–$1,300
Retail Supplies	
Cash register tape	$0–$60
Shopping bags	$0–$400
Gift boxes	$0–$900
Sales tags and/or labels	$0–$150
Office Furniture, Equipment, and Supplies	
Computer system (including printer)	$1,000–$1,500
Fax machine	$100–$250
Two-line full-featured phone system	$70–$80
Voice mail	$6–$20/month
E-mail	$0–$25/month
Website design	$500–$5,000
Website hosting	$50–$500/month
Uninterruptible power supply	$125–$250
Zip drive backup	$150–$300
Surge protector	$15–$60

Estimated Startup Expenses, continued

Item	Price
Calculator	$15–$50
Copier	$300–$1,000
Desk	$200–$600
Desk chair	$60–$200
Printer stand	$50–$75
File cabinet(s) (2-drawer, letter-sized)	$25–$100
Bookcase (4 shelves)	$70
Computer/copier paper	$25–$50
Business cards	$6–$12
Letterhead paper	$30
Matching envelopes	$35
Address stamp or stickers	$10
Extra printer cartridge	$25–$80
Extra fax cartridge	up to $80
Zip drive disks	$45–$120
Mouse pad	$5
Miscellaneous office supplies	$100–$150
Packaging/Shipping Equipment	
Hand truck	$55–$125
High-speed tape dispenser	$16–$25
Carton stapler	$200–$500
Electronic scale	$50–$715
Paper shredder	$25–$125
Packaging/Shipping Supplies	
Sealing tape	$5–$8
Boxes	$225–$400
Mailing labels	$75–$200
Cushioned mailers	$150–$250
Packing materials	$50–$350
Gift Basket Supplies	
Baskets/containers	$400–$4,000
Packing materials	$200–$2,000
Decorative materials	$200–$2,000
Shrink wrap film and/or cellophane	$50–$200
Products/gifts	$750–$20,000
Miscellaneous	$75–$300

Startup Expenses Worksheet

Item	Price
Specialty Equipment	
Work space fixtures	
Work table(s)	
Crafting tools	
Shrink wrapper	
Heat gun	
Company vehicle	
Signage	
Security system	
Storage Fixtures and Hardware	
Storage shelves, cabinets	
Store Equipment/Fixtures (for retail operations)	
Special displays and related hardware	
Display shelving	
Cash register	
Counter	
Marking guns (1 or 2)	
Floor gondolas (5 to 10)	
Pegboard (5 to 10 panels)	
Hooks	
Showcases (1 or 2)	
Wall gondolas (5 to 10)	
Retail Supplies	
Cash register tape	
Shopping bags	
Gift boxes	
Sales tags and/or labels	
Office Furniture, Equipment, and Supplies	
Computer system (including printer)	
Fax machine	
Two-line full-featured phone system	
Voice mail	
E-mail	
Website design	
Website hosting	
Uninterruptible power supply	

Startup Expenses Worksheet, continued

Item	Price
Zip drive backup	
Surge protector	
Calculator	
Copier	
Desk	
Desk chair	
Printer stand	
File cabinet(s) (2-drawer, letter-sized)	
Bookcase (4 shelves)	
Computer/copier paper	
Business cards	
Letterhead paper	
Matching envelopes	
Address stamp or stickers	
Extra printer cartridge	
Extra fax cartridge	
Zip drive disks	
Mouse pad	
Miscellaneous office supplies	
Packaging/Shipping Equipment	
Hand truck	
High-speed tape dispenser	
Carton stapler	
Electronic scale	
Paper shredder	
Packaging/Shipping Supplies	
Sealing tape	
Boxes	
Mailing labels	
Cushioned mailers	
Packing materials	
Gift Basket Supplies	
Baskets/containers	
Packing materials	
Decorative materials	
Shrink wrap film and/or cellophane	
Products/gifts	
Miscellaneous	
TOTAL	

Where Will You Start?
Locating and Setting Up Your Business

The flexibility of a gift basket business gives you a lot of choices in where to locate your operation and how to get it set up. You can opt for a retail store, a warehouse location, or your own home. Regardless of your location, you can sell face -to-face, via mail order, or on the internet—or use a combination of those methods. Though industry surveys indicate that more than half of gift basket businesses have retail locations, the locations of basketeers who participated in the research for this book showed just the opposite—more than half of them are homebased. Solid research is limited, but anecdotal evidence suggests an abundance of successful homebased gift basket operations.

Because of the room required to store inventory and assemble baskets, homebased gift basket businesses will find their growth limited by the available space. Whether or not this is a problem for you depends on your own personal goals. If you are looking to create a sizable company with several employees and generate hundreds of thousands of dollars each year in sales, you'll need a commercial location. But if your goal is a small business that generates a comfortable income for you, being homebased may be the ideal situation. A variety of other business goals and situations fall within those two extremes, so think about what your goals are, then consider your various location options and come up with a compatible solution for your situation.

Going Retail

You have a number of options if you decide to open a retail store. You can locate in a mall, a strip shopping center, a stand-alone store, or a cart or kiosk. Each has its own advantages and disadvantages.

In addition to customers who already know they want gift baskets, retail shops appeal to impulse shoppers and busy professionals. Impulse buyers make unplanned purchases simply because an item appeals to them, and professionals stop to buy an item they need at a convenient place that caters to the person on the run. Capturing either or both of these markets means you have to think about the accessibility of your store, how to display merchandise, and additional products to carry. You also need to consider how you can help your customers make the right selections and get them wrapped, packaged, and delivered as efficiently as possible. (See Appendix C, "Retail Location Checklist," for help in deciding on a location.)

In a retail store, you'll probably want to offer other gift items in addition to baskets, such as glassware, linens, stationery, books, local crafts, dried flowers, collectibles, etc. If they are well-displayed and in keeping with your store's image, they can significantly increase your profits as add-on sales and impulse items.

Among the factors to consider when deciding on a retail location for your business are:

- *Anticipated sales volume.* How will the location contribute to your sales volume? Consider the presence or potential presence of other businesses that will compete with you, and be sure the market is strong enough to support all of you.
- *Accessibility to potential customers.* Consider how easy it will be for customers to get to your business. If vehicle traffic is often heavy, or if the speed limit is more than 35 mph, drivers may have difficulty entering or leaving your site. Narrow

entrances and exits, turns that are hard to negotiate, and parking lots that are always full are deterrents that can prevent would-be customers from patronizing your shop.

If you are relying on strong pedestrian traffic, consider whether or not nearby businesses will generate foot traffic for you. Large department stores will draw many customers and shopping centers in busy office districts might attract pedestrian shoppers, particularly during weekday lunch hours. By contrast, a strip center anchored by a supermarket may not be the best location; grocery shoppers rarely browse through a strip mall either before or after they do their food buying. Claire S. says she learned this the hard way when she and a partner opened their first gift shop in South Florida. The parking lot was always full, but shoppers went directly to the grocery store and back to their cars—they didn't take the time to visit her store. That partnership eventually dissolved, and Claire went on to find a better location for her gift basket business.

Consider the entrance to the site. Is it on the street level or an upper floor? Can it be reached from a main street or is it difficult to find?

Take some time to analyze the site. Monitor foot and auto traffic patterns at different times of the day. See if those patterns fit the hours you want to do business. Visit the prospective site on several different days to assess any changes in the pattern.

- *Rent-paying capacity of your business.* The best locations will usually command the highest rents. If you've done a sales and profit projection for your first year of operation, you will know approximately how much revenue you can expect to generate and you can use that information to decide how much rent you can afford to pay. Of course, it is a catch-22 since higher rent locations also usually generate higher traffic, which should result in higher sales.

- *Restrictive ordinances.* You may encounter unusually restrictive ordinances that make an otherwise strong site less than ideal, such as limitations on

Bright Idea

Consider subleasing space in an existing retail shop. Established retailers already have their target markets defined, their image developed, and a clientele established. But don't jump into a sublease agreement without first studying the operation and being sure you want to be associated with this store and its customers. In turn, be prepared to show the retailer how your presence will be beneficial to the store. This needs to be a win-win situation.

the hours of the day when trucks can legally load or unload. Cities and towns are composed of areas—from a few blocks to many acres in size—zoned only for commercial, industrial, or residential development. Each zone may have further restrictions. A commercial zone may permit one type of business but not another, so check the zoning codes of any potential location before pursuing a specific site or spending a lot of time and money on a market survey.

- *Traffic density.* Modern site analysis distinguishes between automobile and pedestrian traffic. If only auto traffic were important, most businesses would be located near highways or main roads. With careful examination of foot traffic, you can determine the approximate sales potential of each pedestrian passing a given location. Two factors are especially important in this analysis: total

And the Answer Is...

As you analyze the pedestrian traffic at a retail location you're considering, use this as a model for your interviews:

Begin by dressing professionally and carry a clipboard on which you can make notes. Approach people courteously and say, "Excuse me. I'm considering opening a store in this shopping center and I'm trying to decide if this is a good location for my type of business. May I have two minutes of your time to ask a few questions?"

If they refuse, thank them anyway and move on to the next person. However, most people will agree. When they do, quickly ask your questions and let them get on with their business. Make your survey simple; the following questions should tell you what you need to know:

○ What is your primary purpose for being at this shopping center today?
○ Which store or stores have or will you visit?
○ Do you think this shopping center needs a gift basket store?
○ If a gift basket store opened in this location, would you patronize it?

At this point, you have the basic information you need. But if the person is willing to talk, you might want to find out more. If this is the case, then say, "Thank you for answering my questions. Do you have time for three more questions about your gift-buying habits?" If they say yes, ask:

○ If a gift basket store opened in this location, what types of baskets would you be likely to buy?
○ What is your preferred price range for the gift baskets you typically buy?
○ Where do you currently buy your gift baskets and other gift items?

pedestrian traffic during business hours and the percentage of that traffic that's likely to enter your shop.

To make pedestrian traffic counts, select a few half-hour periods during busy hours of the day. You should only count potential customers for your business; total numbers of passersby are not the most significant factor. What you need to know is if these are the types of people who would be shopping for gifts. Why are they at the location at this time? To find out, ask them. Do a brief interview. Ask if they feel there is a need for a gift basket service at the location and find out if they would patronize such a service if it existed. Find out what kinds of baskets they would be interested in buying and where they now shop for most gifts.

Take your sample periods and multiply the results over a week, month, and quarter, and use those figures in your financial forecasts. Certainly this process involves some guessing in your calculations, but if you're careful with your questions and honest with your analysis, you should get a reasonably accurate picture of what to expect.

- *Customer parking facilities.* The site should provide convenient and adequate parking, as well as easy access for customers. Storefront parking is always better than a rear lot; people like to be able to see the parking lot before they turn off the main thoroughfare. The lot should be well-lit and secure. Consider whether the parking area will need expansion, resurfacing, or striping—possibly at an additional cost to you. If you're looking at a freestanding location, think big and envision how you will accommodate the hordes of customers your gift basket business will eventually attract.

- *Proximity to other businesses.* Neighboring businesses may influence your store's volume, and their presence can work for you or against you. Studies of the natural clustering of businesses show that certain types of companies do well when located close to one another. For example, men's and women's apparel and variety stores are commonly located near department stores. Restaurants, barber shops, candy, tobacco, and jewelry stores are often found near theaters. Florists are often grouped with shoe stores and women's clothing stores. For a gift basket service, customers who patronize such places as gourmet food shops, florists, dry cleaners, shoe and apparel stores, and coffee/candy or other specialty shops are also prospects for your business.

> **Bright Idea**
> Even if you decide to open a retail shop, you may choose to maintain an office in your home to maximize your shop space. Use this area for bookkeeping, marketing activities, order-taking, and any other business activity that doesn't require face-to-face contact with customers.

- *History of the site.* Find out the recent history of each site under consideration before you make a final selection. Who were the previous tenants and why are they no longer there? There are sites—in malls and shopping centers, as well as in freestanding locations—that have been occupied by successions of business failures. The reasons for the failures may be completely unrelated to the success potential of your gift basket shop, or they could mean your business will meet the same fate. You need to study and understand why previous tenants failed so you can avoid their mistakes.

- *Terms of the lease.* Be sure you understand all the details of the lease, because it's possible an excellent site may have unacceptable leasing terms. The time to negotiate terms is before you sign the lease; don't wait until you've moved in to try to change the terms.

Lease Lingo

Everything has its own language, and the world of leasing is no exception. Here are a few terms to understand while considering and negotiating a lease.

Flat lease: This lease is for a set price for a set period of time. In a lease like this, you would want to get the longest term possible. Although more and more scarce, having a flat lease allows you to really predict this large operating expense.

Step lease: This lease has built-in increases, often annually, throughout the life of the lease. Step leases aren't even that great for landlords because they are merely estimating cost increases. Be sure to review these very carefully before signing on the dotted line.

Net lease: This covers the landlord's concerns about the step lease by increasing the lease only when cost increases occur. This can be very unpredictable and make your lease cost estimating very difficult. You can avoid some of that pain by insisting on capping increases in a given time period and other possible cost-containing clauses. Keep in mind, it is usually to the landlord's advantage to retain you as a lessee, so don't feel like the cards are always stacked in the landlord's favor.

Percentage lease: An interesting lease arrangement, this lease typically involves a base amount plus a percentage of your gross revenue. Although this can work in your favor, in that your lease expense is directly related to how well your business is doing, it does mean a bit more work for you since you will need to provide sales records.

- *Rent-advertising relationship.* You may need to account for up to six months of advertising and promotion expenditures in your working capital. Few businesses can succeed without any sales promotion, and the larger the sum you can afford for well-placed, well-targeted advertising and promotions, the greater your chances of success.

The amount you plan to spend on advertising may be closely related to your site choice and the proposed rent. If you locate in a shopping center or mall supported by huge ad budgets and the presence of large, popular chain and department stores, you will most likely generate revenue from the first day you open your doors—with no individual advertising at all. Of course, your rental expenses will be proportionately higher than those for an independent location.

If you do not locate in an area that attracts a lot of foot traffic, you will experience a slower growth rate, even if your business fronts a high-traffic street. Your real profits will come as you develop a clientele—and this will require advertising and promotion. Both center developers and tenants recommend that operators just starting out begin in small community centers and then graduate to larger regional centers or malls.

Before signing on the dotted line to lease a site, review the "Real Estate Lease Checklist" in Appendix C.

Additional Retail Options

An alternative to a traditional retail store is a cart or kiosk. Carts and kiosks are a great way to test your business before moving into a regular store, or they could be a permanent part of your operating strategy. One of the hottest trends in mall retailing is the temporary tenant—a retailer that comes into a mall, sometimes in a store but often on a cart or kiosk, for a specified period, usually to capture holiday or seasonal sales. You could, for example, have a retail cart that you set up in a local mall around Valentine's Day, Easter, Mother's Day, and Christmas, and work out of your home the remainder of the year.

If you have a retail store, a temporary cart at another location can generate immediate sales and serve as a marketing tool for your year-round location.

Renting cart or kiosk space is usually significantly less than the rent for an in-line (traditional) store, but rates vary dramatically depending on the location and season. Mall space in particular can be pricey. For example, rent in a class C mall during an off-peak season may cost as little as $400 per month for cart space, but a class A mall in December might charge $4,000 to $5,000 per month for the same amount of space.

Carts can be leased or purchased. New carts can be purchased for $3,000 to $5,000; monthly lease fees typically run 8 percent to 12 percent of the new price. You

> **Bright Idea**
>
> Ask the manager of a large office building if you can set up a special table in the lobby for Secretaries' Day or Boss's Day. Most will let you do it for free as a service to their tenants; some may charge a small fee. Assemble a selection of affordable baskets and have gift cards available. Bring along a helper who can deliver the baskets as you sell them.

can probably get a good deal on a used cart; just be sure it will suit your needs. If a used cart needs significant modifications to work for you, it may be better to buy new and get exactly what you need.

Though kiosks are often occupied by temporary tenants, they have a greater sense of permanency than carts. They typically offer more space and more design flexibility. They're also more expensive—expect to pay $9,000 to $10,000 or more to purchase a new kiosk. As with carts, you may be able to lease a kiosk, although there are not as many available, or you can buy a used kiosk.

Carts and kiosks are available from a variety of sources. Manufacturers and brokers advertise in a variety of retail trade publications, or you can contact the manufacturers listed in Appendix A. But before you invest in a cart or kiosk, decide where you're going to put it. Many malls have restrictions on the size and design of temporary tenant facilities, or they want all such fixtures to look alike.

Playing and Working Fair

You can also sell your baskets at fairs and festivals, which is a primary market for Melissa B., a homebased basketeer in Willow Hill, Pennsylvania. She sets up a booth at all kinds of outdoor events. Her primary criterion is that the show be within a 50-mile radius of her home so that she can comfortably service the follow-up business she gets.

Some fairs and festivals provide tents for exhibitors; others do not. Check this out in advance, because you don't want to sit—or have your products displayed—in hot, direct sunlight all day. Small shade tents can be purchased at garden stores and special-event equipment companies. Bring one to three tables (depending on the size of the table and the size of your space) to display your baskets on, one or two chairs, and a locking cash box. It's also a good idea to bring a small cooler with snacks and beverages. The cost of renting space at fairs and festivals typically ranges from $100 to $300 per event, depending on the size, location, and length of the event. Unless the show is brand new, organizers will be able to provide you with detailed information on setup requirements and what you can expect in the way of customer traffic.

The type of show dictates what Melissa takes in the way of products. At flea and craft markets, for example, people are looking for bargains and perhaps even supplies to make their own baskets. At those shows, she stocks her booth with lower-priced gift baskets and a selection of plain baskets, plus plenty of brochures and business cards. It's an inexpensive way, she says, to get her name out to hundreds, and sometimes thousands, of prospective customers.

At the more upscale shows and festivals, she'll take dried flower arrangements and higher-priced gift baskets, along with a smaller supply of plain baskets—and, as always, lots of brochures and cards. "I try to find out who they're buying for," Melissa says. "If they're buying for themselves, I give them a brochure and card, and say, 'By the way, if you know anybody who is getting married or having a baby, these will make great gifts.' If they're buying as a gift, I tell them I have some plain baskets if they're interested in decorating their home."

> **Bright Idea**
>
> For a schedule of events that could be promotional or exhibit opportunities for your business, check your local telephone directory— many include a calendar in the consumer information section up front. The local chamber of commerce should also be able to provide you with a list of community events.

The Home Advantage

The decision to set up your business at home will depend on a number of things, including local zoning codes, your landlord (if you have one), your family situation, your budget, and your own plans for how you want to operate your company.

A particular challenge to operating a homebased gift basket business is that it takes up a lot of room. Compared to many other types of homebased businesses, it's inventory-intensive and requires a substantial work area that has the potential to get pretty messy. No matter how neat and organized you are or try to be, when you're assembling baskets, it's inevitable that streamers, ribbon, cellophane, straw, and various other inventory items will be strewn through your work area—and the more baskets you make per day, the bigger the mess will be.

If you're going to operate from home, you need a work area (see the "Getting Ready to Work" section on page 75), storage space, and some administrative space. Your garage or a spare bedroom will probably be enough to get you started.

The most obvious advantage of being homebased, especially in the beginning, is the small initial capital outlay. The money you might otherwise have spent on leasing commercial space can be invested in your inventory or marketing efforts.

A homebased business also offers substantial tax breaks, but you must be sure your setup meets IRS requirements. According to *The Ernst & Young Tax Guide* (John Wiley & Sons), the IRS says that certain expenses are deductible if part of your home is "your principal place of business for any trade or business in which you engage, or [it is] a place to meet or deal with your patients, clients, or customers in the normal course of your trade or business." But you must choose a room—not just a corner of a room—to use solely as your office and/or workroom. If it also contains a TV or stereo and serves as a den or guest room, or if you assemble baskets on the dining room table, your home office deduction probably will not hold up under an IRS audit.

What can you deduct? Directly related expenses, which are expenses that benefit only the business part of your home, and a portion of indirect expenses, which are the costs involved in keeping up and running your entire home. For example, your office furniture and equipment are fully deductible as directly related expenses. In the area of indirect expenses, you may deduct a portion of your household utilities and services (electric, gas, water, sewage, trash collection, etc.) based on the percentage of space you use for business purposes. Other examples of indirect expenses include real estate taxes, deductible mortgage interest, casualty losses, rent, insurance, repairs, security systems, and depreciation.

Before you invest too much time in planning or setting up a homebased operation, check your local zoning codes. Many municipalities have ordinances that limit the nature and volume of commercial activities that can occur in residential areas. Some outright prohibit the establishment of homebased businesses. Others may allow such enterprises but place restrictions regarding issues such as signage, traffic, employees, commercially marked vehicles, and noise. Find out what, if any, ordinances are in place regarding homebased businesses before applying for your business license; you may need to adjust your plan to be in compliance. Call your local city hall's general information number and ask to be referred to the appropriate department—usually the planning and zoning department, or perhaps the business and occupational licensing office. Don't ask the clerk for advice; instead, get a copy of any ordinances concerning homebased businesses and the specific zoning code that applies to your property. You may need to consult an attorney who can interpret the fine points of the ordinance. Also, there is often a substantial difference between what an ordinance says and the way it is enforced.

If your business will violate the zoning code, you may still be able to operate by applying for a variance or conditional-use permit. Or you can apply to have the zoning changed. Both of these processes are lengthy and require a significant amount of documentation, so you should seriously consider everything involved before you begin the process.

Mail Order

Setting up a mail order operation makes the entire world your market. You can take orders over the phone, by mail, by fax, or on the internet and ship the basket virtually anywhere. You can choose to operate exclusively as a mail order business, or use mail order in addition to a retail or business-to-business service.

Your Primary Sales Tool

The foundation of any mail order business is a strong catalog and other direct-mail marketing pieces, such as fliers, brochures, and sales letters. Even in the internet age, mail order retailers are finding print catalogs to still be not only viable but important sales tools. At a cost of approximately $10,000, Chris K.'s catalog accounted for two-thirds of her overall startup expenses—but she sells nationwide from her California homebased office. Sharon M. sees the money she spends on high-quality brochures as money she's not spending on rent for a retail store and display area in high-priced New York.

Unless you have direct experience with graphic arts and design, hire a professional to create the format and handle all the prepress arrangements for your brochures and catalogs. Be sure your photography is top-notch—it is, after all, the only visual image your customers will have of your product. The copy needs to be more than just a listing of each basket's contents; consider hiring a professional writer experienced in direct-mail copy.

The All-Important Mailing List

You'll develop your customer base by mailing your catalog or brochure to people who fit your target market profile. How do you find these folks? The easiest way is to buy mailing lists. As you probably know from the amount of marketing mail you receive yourself, developing, maintaining, and selling mailing lists is a big business. The companies that maintain these lists can provide you with names and addresses of potential customers who fall into your desired demographics.

Buying a list can be expensive, so take the time to do it right. Contact several list brokers before making a decision. Find out what guarantees they offer. Ask how they acquire data and what techniques are in place to ensure the accuracy and currency of the information. In today's mobile society, a list that's even one year old will likely contain a sizeable percentage of names of people who have moved. Ask for the list broker's references and check them before making a final selection.

Once you've found a good list broker, stick with them. A good broker is a valuable partner in growing a mail order business because you'll always be trying new lists, even after you're established and profitable.

Smart Tip

Tip...

Whenever you try a new list, test the potential response by mailing to a small segment before you spend the money on mailing to the entire list.

Dollar Stretcher

Ask your suppliers about possible co-op advertising money. This is when they contribute to the cost of your catalog from their advertising budget because their products are prominently mentioned.

Your most valuable list will be your in-house list—the people who have become your customers. You need to frequently mail information to people on this list and be creative when developing ideas for ways they can purchase more gift baskets. See Chapter 9 for techniques successful basketeers are already using, then let your imagination help you come up with even more.

As this list grows, you'll find handling it a complex, time-consuming, and critical task. Consider hiring an outside company to take over your database management. After all, you're starting a gift basket business because you love creating baskets; if you're an expert at database management, perhaps you should consider starting a company offering that service.

Packing and Shipping Tips

Unless the basket is for a particular event and the customer has requested delayed shipping, get your orders out the door and on their way as quickly as possible. People want immediate gratification. The faster you deliver, the more orders you'll get.

Package your baskets with extreme care, and be sure the exterior of the box can take a serious beating without damaging the contents. No matter how many "fragile" and "handle with care" stickers you affix to the outside, you can be assured that while it's in transit, the box will be shaken, turned upside down, and tossed, and have things stacked on top of it—that's simply the nature of the shipping business.

For more information on setting up and running a mail order operation, see Entrepreneur's business startup guide *Start Your Own Mail Order Business*.

The Useful Website

You will read more about web sales in Chapter 10, but it is worth mentioning here that no matter how you set up your business—as a retail operation or solely as a mail order business—your website can drive business. And conversely, a website allows you to operate in cyberspace without a retail location and perhaps even without a print catalog, but you still need a physical space to warehouse the items you use to create your baskets and work space to create the baskets and package them for shipping.

Nonretail Commercial Space

If you don't want to—or simply don't have the room to—operate from home, but you don't want to build a retail business, consider taking space in a warehouse or light industrial facility.

If your inventory includes temperature-sensitive items, such as foods and candles, be sure the facility is adequately air-conditioned. Also, thoroughly research security and accessibility issues, especially if you expect to be working late at night or on weekends.

Consignment Sales

You might want to consider selling your baskets in other retail outlets on a consignment basis. Under this arrangement, you would supply ready-made baskets to retailers—typically small specialty shops for which you create baskets in their area of specialization—who would then display them in their stores. If the baskets sell, you split the profits, usually on a 50-50 basis (note: you don't split the *selling price* but what you make over and above your costs of products and the basket).

Consignment sales give you free display space, broaden your potential customer base, and allow you more time to make your baskets. The best prospects for this type of venture include stores that sell gourmet foods, bath products, gifts, exotic imports, handmade crafts, tourist souvenirs, and similar items. If you create specialty baskets targeted to specific hobbies—such as golfers, tennis players, campers, dancers, etc.—approach the specialty stores that cater to these consumers. Each basket should

Order in the House

Even as a mail order business, you have the option of offering standard or custom baskets. In either case, accuracy on the part of the order taker is essential; a mistake can cost you hundreds of dollars in replacement costs and reshipping fees, not to mention the priceless value of lost future sales and goodwill. Whether you use an outside fulfillment service to process orders or handle this yourself, be sure everyone who talks to your customers has been thoroughly trained on your product line and is prepared to represent you and project the image you have created.

include your company name and contact information so the buyer and recipient can contact you for future orders.

Once your business is established, carefully examine your consignment agreement to see if it is going to be beneficial in the long run. If it isn't, end the arrangement. There's no reason to continue to share your profits if you don't need to.

Displaying Merchandise

In any retail operation, whether it's a store, a cart, a kiosk, or a temporary booth at a festival, you need to use your display space creatively and effectively.

The image you want to project is a major consideration in how you display your merchandise. Will your gift basket store appeal only to upscale customers, or do you want to have gifts for just about every imaginable price range? The image your shop projects will have a lot to do with who comes in to find out what you're offering.

Because gift baskets are generally perceived as upscale gift items, if you want to reach a broader market, you'll need to project the image that you carry something for everyone right from the start by placing a range of baskets in plain sight. This will help attract a wider customer base. You should also highlight at least one or two corporate-looking baskets to draw the executive or businessperson who may be shopping for something else but realizes your shop is a convenient place to find a perfect business gift either now or in the future.

In a store, line the walls with shelving that extends about 6 feet up the walls. In the central floor area, set up displays using tables, racks, and gondolas, which are island units with back-to-back open shelving.

To evaluate your display, stand a few feet from the entrance to your store and look at it through the eyes of a first-time shopper. Ask yourself:

- Does the in-store advertising grab you from a distance?
- Do the displays at the front of the store make a clear statement about the type of products you carry?
- Is there a natural and logical flow to the traffic pattern in and out of the store? In other words, when people step into the store, will they feel at ease moving from one display to another, or will they have a sense of barriers that might keep them from shopping comfortably?
- Have you addressed the customer's visual point of reference from the top of the store to the floor? When they look around, what are they seeing? Though your eye-level displays are certainly the most critical, don't get lazy about the rest of your displays and the store's general appearance.
- Are there clear, wide aisles for customers to browse comfortably and for salespeople to keep an eye on customers for service—and to prevent shoplifting?

Locate your checkout counter at the entrance to your shop. Though you need a clear space to ring up and wrap purchases, use the area around and behind the counter to display last-minute and impulse-purchase items. Also display notices of upcoming holiday or special occasion baskets that you will have available.

Getting Ready to Work

Set up your production area in the way that works best for you. Of course, you'll want to arrange things to provide maximum efficiency, so don't put an item you'll reach for 10 times a day on a shelf that you need a stool to reach.

Though your basket assembly area may not be large enough to store all of your inventory, it should hold a substantial amount so you don't waste a lot of time moving items around. Place shelving along the walls for gift items and install large hooks for hanging baskets.

Sue C., the basketeer in Salt Lake City, keeps an office in her house but has her production area set up in a small warehouse. The walls are lined with cupboards and shelves, where her inventory is stored. In the center of the room is a long counter that functions as a production line—by being in the center, nothing is very far from reach. Products and supplies are arranged in a very systematic way, with plenty of thought given to easy access. Rolls of cellophane, wires, and ribbons hang above the work table. Under the table are bins of plain fill material for the basket bottom and decorative fill for the visible areas. Neatly arranged on the counter are scissors, knives, staple guns, tape, glue guns, and other tools necessary to assemble the baskets. Most of the counter area is kept clear for basket assembly.

In Commack, New York, Christine M. operates exclusively from home, using a large room for production. Like Sue, she has lined the walls with shelves for her inventory. However, she has three work tables instead of just one—one for assembling the basket, a second for wrapping it, and the third for preparing it for shipping.

Your office area needs to support your personal work style while allowing you to attend to all the necessary administrative functions of your business. You'll need a desk, a comfortable chair, a place to put supplies (one gift basket business owner uses a rolltop desk and puts her stamps, stickers, envelopes, and other supplies in all the cubbyholes), and filing cabinets.

> **Tip...**
>
> **Smart Tip**
>
> If you have customers outside your local area, hang wall clocks set to their time zones in your office. You'll be able to see what time it is where they are at a glance, rather than having to do the calculation in your head before you place a call or leave a message.

Should You Buy an Existing Operation?

If you find the startup process a bit overwhelming, you may think taking over an existing gift basket retail facility or similar operation seems like a simple shortcut to getting into your own gift basket business. It can be, but you must proceed with extreme caution.

You can find stores for sale advertised in trade publications, shopping center publications, and your local newspaper. You might also want to check with a business broker—they're listed in the Yellow Pages of your telephone directory—to see what they have available.

Buyers frequently purchase shops "lock, stock, and barrel," including store fixtures, equipment, inventory, and supplies. Others negotiate for portions of these items, preferring to remain free to create their own inventory and image.

Take care that you do not select a store that is already doomed, perhaps by a poor location or the unfavorable reputation of the former owner. Especially in the case of the latter, it's much easier to start with a clean slate than to try to clean up after someone else. Before buying an existing business, take the following steps:

- *Find out why the business is for sale.* Many entrepreneurs sell thriving businesses because they're ready to do something else or they want to retire. Others will try to sell a declining business in the hopes of cutting their losses.

- *Do a thorough site analysis to determine if the location is suitable for a gift basket business.* Has damaging competition moved in since the business originally opened?

- *Examine the store's financial records for the last three years, and for the current year to date.* Compare sales tax records with the owner's claims.

- *Sit in on the store's operation for a few days, observing daily business volume and clientele.* See for yourself how closely the reality of the day-to-day operation matches the seller's claims.

- *Evaluate the worth of existing store fixtures.* They must be in good condition and consistent with your plans for store image and merchandise.

- *Determine the costs of remodeling and redecorating if the store's décor is to be changed.* Will these costs negate the advantage of buying?

- *Decide how much of the existing inventory will suit your plan.* Most sellers deplete their inventory to lower the store's price. Even so, any undesirable stock is a waste of your money.

When Sue C. decided to start her own gift basket business, she first went to a business broker looking for an existing company to buy. She was disappointed in what was available, but did find one gift basket business that looked moderately promising. After studying the proposed deal herself, she consulted her advisors. Her accountant asked what her plans for the business were.

After she detailed all the changes and improvements she intended to make, he said, "It sounds like you're going to spend $30,000 buying something that you want to change 70 percent of. You have enough energy and enough contacts—why not do it yourself? Start your own business and do it your way from the beginning."

Be sure any business you're considering buying is worth the price. If you're going to make substantial changes, it may make more sense to start from scratch. But if you decide to buy, include a noncompete clause in your contract so the seller doesn't go out and start a competing operation in your service area. And remember that no seller can guarantee that the customers they have when they sell you the business will stick around.

See the "Business Evaluation Checklist" in Appendix C.

Business Opportunity or Franchise

Another alternative to starting from scratch on your own is to purchase a business opportunity or franchise. Many people do very well with this route, but there are significant risks involved.

What Is a Franchise?

Franchising is a method of marketing a product or service within a structure dictated by the franchisor. When you buy a franchise, you are entering into an agreement either to distribute products or operate under a format identified with and structured by the parent company. One major advantage of franchising is that you have the opportunity to buy into a product or system that is established, rather than having to create everything yourself. There is, of course, a price to pay—in addition to your startup equipment and inventory, you'll have to pay a franchise fee. Also, most franchise companies collect ongoing royalties, usually a percentage of your gross sales. They do, however, provide you with ongoing support.

You may want to look for a specific gift basket franchise or a gift or retail franchise that incorporates gift baskets into a larger product line. For example, Balloons and Bears describes itself as a "5-in-1 gift shop" offering flowers, gift baskets, balloons, bears, and greeting cards. Candy Bouquet is a candy and gourmet chocolate store offering floral-type arrangements of candy—arrangements that are as much fun and require as much creativity as most gift baskets.

Franchises are regulated by the Federal Trade Commission (FTC) and by a number of states. Thoroughly research any franchise you are considering and expect the franchisor to want to know a lot about you, too. After all, if you're going to be responsible for operating under their name, they'll want to be sure you'll do it right.

Check It Out

Protect your investment by thoroughly checking out any franchise or business opportunity before you pay any money.

○ *Ask plenty of questions.* Find out about the quality of the products, whether or not the prices are competitive, how much you are expected to buy, and if the company will assist you with promotions.

○ *Find out how long the company has been in business.* Are they equipped to meet the demands of a growing market?

○ *Ask about how your alliance with the company works.* Is it a one-shot deal or an ongoing relationship? Under what terms and conditions can your contract be modified or terminated?

○ *Get everything in writing and verify as much as possible.*

○ *Do the basic arithmetic.* How long will it take to recoup your initial investment? Equally important, how long is it likely to take before you begin making real profits?

○ *Ask for and check references from people who have already purchased the opportunity.*

○ *Call regulatory agencies and business associations.* Check with your state's division of consumer services, your attorney general's office, a regional FTC office, your local chamber of commerce, and the Better Business Bureau to see if they have any information or complaints on file.

○ *Visit the corporate office and attend company shows and sales meetings.*

○ *Don't be pressured into making a quick decision.* Buying a business shouldn't be an impulse purchase.

○ *Be alert to signs of possible fraud.* Be wary of claims of extraordinarily high or guaranteed profits or of promises that you can make lots of money with little work. Compare the initial fee you're asked to pay with the fair market value of the products, supplies, or training you'll receive, and question any serious variances.

Franchise Pros

There are many good reasons to open a franchise operation:

• *Reduced failure risk.* If the franchise is well-run, its operators are likely to be successful with their businesses as well.

• *Turnkey operation.* Typically, the franchise provides marketing materials, makes it easy for you to purchase the right supplies, and either provides things like signage or at least provides all the designs for signage, store layout, etc. so you don't need to spend time dealing with all of that.

- *Standardized products and systems.* No need to invent your own ways of doing paperwork, buying, and other operations—the franchise tells you how they want it done.

- *Collective buying power.* The franchisor can buy for all its franchises, making the price as good as it gets considering the quantities they can buy in comparison to what you would be doing on your own.

- *Supervision and consulting.* The franchisor acts as an automatic consultant, offering advice, training, and problem solving. After all, it is to their advantage for you to be successful.

- *National and local advertising programs.* Think of McDonald's, Subway, KFC, the kings of franchising. They do generic advertising that benefits all their franchisees (for which you contribute a share!), and can advertise in markets that you would never be able to afford on your own. For a gift basket business, this could mean the difference between having national accounts or just local business.

- *Point-of-sale advertising.* A gift basket franchise will most likely be an operation with a storefront. This point-of-sale advertising material can be provided by the company.

- *Uniform packaging.* No need to worry about the packaging you need to box up your standard line of baskets; the franchisor has all that worked out!

Franchise Cons

There are dozens of other reasons to consider a franchise operation—possible financial assistance, an operations manual, sales and marketing assistance—but there are also many cons to the franchise route, including:

- *Loss of control.* You always have someone else telling you how to do things. And you have to listen.

- *Expensive.* Franchising can be an expensive route to take. Not only do you need upfront money, but there are royalty fees of anywhere from 2 to 6 percent of your sales each month.

- *A binding contract.* You must sign an agreement with the franchisor, which will lock you into the franchise for a specified period. Be sure to read the restrictions carefully, especially about how to get out of the franchise.

- *Collective problems.* Just like the collective success of the franchise, you are also part of the collective problems. If a fellow franchise owner delivers a basket with a cockroach in it and it makes national news, the news will be about "Joe's Baskets," which includes you.

- *Curtailed creativity.* Most franchises require you do things their way, with little leeway to be creative. In a business like gift baskets, which you may have gotten into because you enjoy being creative, this may be a deal killer.

What Is a Business Opportunity?

A company that asks for a substantial initial payment in exchange for assistance in starting your own business and/or wants to sell you inventory required to carry on your business may be selling a business opportunity. Business opportunities are regulated to a degree on a national level by the FTC and in at least 25 states by state consumer protection legislation. But because of the broad scope of business opportunities, they are not always easy to identify and not all of them are covered by regulations.

The advantages of business opportunities are very similar to those of franchises. They provide a vehicle for getting into business for yourself within an established structure and, in theory at least, with the support of a parent company that knows the ropes.

Though many business opportunities are legitimate, many others are offered by companies that are either unable to fulfill their promises for various reasons or never had any intention of doing so in the first place. In fact, there are few transactions in which the phrase "buyer beware" is more important than when purchasing a business opportunity.

You can find business opportunities literally everywhere—advertised in magazines, newspapers, on television infomercials, and at trade shows, and promoted through one-on-one networking. Though most publishers attempt to screen ads for potential fraud, you should never depend exclusively on the credibility of a publication or other promotional source to determine the validity of a business opportunity. Check it out thoroughly on your own.

Melissa B. started her company with the gift basket business opportunity available through The Basket Connection. She considered several before making her decision. "I had looked for about six years, so I had run the gamut when it came down to hearing what people had to say, their sales pitches, and whatnot," she says. "The one thing I would advise others to look for is somebody you feel you can trust wholeheartedly. And you want to feel proud to tell someone you bought the opportunity." Melissa says that when she called people that some business opportunities had provided as references, she got the impression they felt ashamed about having bought the program in question, perhaps because they realized after the fact that it wasn't a good decision.

So do your homework, and listen to your intuition. When your research and emotions are at odds, keep on researching until you're comfortable. When they agree, you've probably found the right solution.

Human Resources

The People Side of Your Company

Chances are you want to start a gift basket business for two primary reasons: You enjoy the creative aspects of making the baskets and you want to run your own company. Many successful gift basket business owners often deliberately keep their companies as one-person operations because they don't want to deal with the headaches that growth brings. While there's nothing wrong with this strategy, it puts a tremendous amount of pressure on the owner, who may find herself working 12 hours a day, six days a week, during peak seasons.

If your goal is growth, you will reach a point where you must hire people. And even if your goal isn't growth, there may be times when you need help, so it's important to understand the basics of finding, hiring, and managing personnel.

The first step is to decide exactly what you want someone to do. The job description doesn't have to be as formal as one you might expect from a large corporation, but it needs to clearly outline the person's duties and responsibilities. It should also

You Deserve a Break Today

No matter how much you enjoy your work, you need an occasional break from it. This is a particular challenge for solo operators, but it's critical. You need to be able to be away from your operation occasionally, not only for vacations but also for business reasons, such as attending conferences and trade shows. Also, you need a plan in place in case of illness, an accident, or other emergencies.

If you take a long weekend or just one or two days off, with proper planning, your customers won't even know you were gone. For longer periods away, you have two choices: Find someone you can trust who will run the business for you in your absence, or just close temporarily. Sue C. prefers to close when she takes extended time off. In the past, she had someone handle her business, but things didn't get done to her standards and she lost a few customers. Her customers would rather wait for her to return than get substandard service from someone else. "Every customer waits for me to get back to send their baskets out," Sue says.

With a staff to depend on, taking a vacation is easier—just be sure your people are well-trained and committed to maintaining your service levels when you aren't there.

Try these vacation-planning tips on for size:

○ *Plan ahead.* Schedule your vacation time far enough in advance that you can plan your workload around your time off.

○ *Build a backup network.* Look for people you trust who can handle work that can't wait while you're gone, such as sympathy baskets and last-minute orders.

○ *Notify your regular customers.* About two weeks before you leave, tell the customers with whom you communicate regularly that you'll be unavailable so they can place any upcoming orders before you go.

list any special skills or other required credentials, such as a valid driver's license and clean driving record for someone who is going to do deliveries for you.

Next, you need to establish a pay scale. For most of the tasks involved in a gift basket business—assembling baskets, handling shipping and receiving, taking orders, customer service, general cleanup, and making deliveries—expect to pay between $8 and $12 per hour, depending on the size of your business, the specific tasks involved, and average pay scales in your particular market. You should expect to pay more if you hire someone who is a skilled designer. In addition to their hourly rate, consider giving employees production bonuses or some other performance-related incentive.

You should also have a job application form. You can get a basic form at most office supply stores, or you can create your own. No matter which one you choose, have your attorney review the form you will be using for compliance with the most current employment laws.

Every prospective employee should fill out an application—even if it's someone you already know, and even if they've submitted a detailed resume. A resume is not a signed, sworn statement acknowledging that you can fire them if they lie; the application is. The application will also help you verify their resumes; compare the two and make sure the information is consistent.

Now you're ready to start looking for candidates.

Look in the Right Places

Picture the ideal candidate in your mind. Is this person likely to be unemployed and reading the classified ads? It's possible, but you will probably improve your chances for a successful hire if you're more creative in your searching techniques than simply writing a "help wanted" ad.

Sources for prospective employees include vendors, customers (use caution here; you don't want to lose a client because you stole an employee), and professional associations. Check with nearby colleges and perhaps even high schools for part-time help. Put the word out among your social contacts as well—you never know who else might know the perfect person for your company.

Consider using a temporary help or employment agency. Many small businesses shy away from agencies because they feel like they can't afford the fee—but if the agency handles the advertising, initial screening, and background checks, their fee may be well worth paying.

Use caution if you decide to hire friends and relatives—many personal relationships have not been strong enough to survive an employee-employer situation. Christine M., the basketeer in Commack, New York, handles her business alone during most of the year, but hires part-time help for the Christmas holiday season. Most of her employees have been family members who, she says, are very dedicated. Utah gift basket business owner Sue C. also uses her family—her daughters, in particular—to help out during busy times, and says she's never had a problem. But other small business owners tell of nightmarish experiences when a friend or relative refused to accept direction or in other ways abused a personal relationship in the course of business.

In her Florida retail shop, Claire S. has a staff that fluctuates from four to eight people, depending on the time of year. She's hired friends, relatives, and strangers over the years, and says the key to success as an employer is making it clear from the start that you are the one in charge. You don't need to act like a dictator, of course. Be diplomatic, but set the ground rules in advance, and stick to them.

Evaluating Applicants

What kinds of people make good employees for gift basket businesses? It depends on what you want them to do. If you're hiring a delivery person, then you need someone with a good driving record who knows the city. If you're hiring someone to help with administrative tasks, they need to understand the computer and be able to learn your operating system. If you're hiring someone to make baskets, they need to be both creative and able to follow instructions. What is really important is that the people you hire are committed to giving you their best effort during the time they're working so that your customers receive the best service.

When you actually begin the hiring process, don't be surprised if you're as nervous at the prospect of interviewing potential employees as they are about being interviewed. After all, they may need a job—but the future of your company is at stake.

It's a good idea to prepare your interview questions in advance. Develop open-ended questions that encourage the candidate to talk. In addition to knowing what they've done, you want to find out how they did it. Ask each candidate the same set of questions, and make notes as they respond so you can make an accurate assessment and comparison later.

If you're hiring people to assemble baskets, ask them to demonstrate their skills so you can see exactly what they do. Let them put together a standard basket to see how well they follow instructions; then let them design a basket from a description they might receive from a customer.

> **Smart Tip**
>
> According to *Gift Basket Review* magazine, the average gift basket business employs five full-time people, including the owner(s), and four and a half part-time employees.

When the interview is over, let the candidate know what to expect. Is it going to take you several weeks to interview other candidates, check references, and make a decision? Will you want the top candidates to return for a second interview? Will you call the candidate, or should they call you? This is not only a good business practice; it's also just simple common courtesy.

Always check former employers and personal references. Though many companies are very restrictive as to what information they'll verify, you may be surprised at what you can find out. Certainly you should at least confirm that the applicant told the truth about dates and positions held. Personal references are likely to give you some additional insight into the general character and personality of the candidate; this will help you decide if they'll fit into your operation.

Be sure to document every step of the interview and reference-checking process. Even very small companies are finding themselves targets of employment discrimination suits; good records are your best defense if it happens to you.

Once They're on Board

The hiring process is only the beginning of the challenge of having employees. The next thing you need to do is train them.

Many small businesses conduct their "training" just by throwing someone into the job, but that's not fair to the employee, and it's certainly not good for your business. And if you think you can't afford to spend time on training, think again—can you afford not to adequately train your employees? Do you really want them interacting with your customers when you have not told them how you want things done?

In an ideal world, employees could be hired already knowing everything they need to know. But this isn't an ideal world, and if you want the job done right, you have to teach your people how to do it.

Stat Fact
Consider hiring a part- or full-time artist. Claire S. has an artist on her staff who personalizes ceramic gift items with special drawings or paintings, as well as the recipient's name, to make the gift truly unique.

Whether done in a formal classroom setting or on the job, effective training begins with a clear goal and a plan for reaching it. Training will fall into one of three major categories: orientation, which includes explaining company policies and procedures; job skills, which focuses on how to do specific tasks; and ongoing development, which enhances the basic job skills and grooms employees for future challenges and opportunities. The following tips will help maximize your training efforts:

Got It Covered

In most states, if you have three or more employees, you are required by law to carry workers' compensation insurance. This coverage pays medical expenses and replaces a portion of the employee's wages if he or she is injured on the job. Even if you have only one or two employees, you may want to consider this coverage to protect both them and you in the event of an accident.

Details and requirements vary by state; contact your state's insurance office or your own insurance agent for information so you can be sure you're in compliance.

- *Find out how people learn best.* Delivering training is not a one-size-fits-all proposition. People absorb and process information differently, so your training method needs to be compatible with their individual preferences. Some people can read a manual, others prefer a verbal explanation, and still others need to see a demonstration. In a group training situation, your best strategy is to use a combination of methods; when you're working one-on-one, tailor your delivery to fit the needs of the person you're training.

  With some employees, figuring out how they learn best can be a simple matter of asking them. Others may not be able to tell you because they don't understand it themselves. In those cases, experiment with various training styles and see what works best for the specific employee.

- *Use simulation and role-playing to train, practice, and reinforce.* One of the most effective training techniques is simulation, which involves showing an employee how to do something, then allowing them to practice it in a safe, controlled environment. If the task includes interpersonal skills, let the employee role-play with a co-worker to practice what they should say and do in various situations.

- *Be a strong role model.* Don't expect more from your employees than you are willing to do. You're a good role model when you do things the way they should be done, all the time. Don't take shortcuts you don't want your employees to take, and don't behave in any way that you don't want them to behave. On the other hand, don't assume that simply doing things the right way is enough to teach others how to do things. Role modeling is not a substitute for training—it reinforces training. If you only act as a role model but never train others to be one, employees aren't likely to get the message.

- *Look for training opportunities.* Once you get beyond basic orientation and job-skills training, you need to constantly be on the lookout for opportunities to enhance the skill and performance level of your people.

- *Make it real.* Whenever possible, use real-life situations to train—but avoid letting customers know they've become a training experience for employees.

- *Anticipate questions.* Don't assume employees know what to ask. In a new situation, people often don't understand enough to ask questions. Anticipate their questions and answer them in advance.

Bright Idea

Training employees—even part-time, temporary help—to understand your way of doing things is extremely important. These people are representing your company and they need to know how to maintain the image and standards you have worked hard to establish.

- *Ask for feedback.* Encourage employees to let you know how you're doing as a trainer. Just as you evaluate their performance, convince them that it's OK to tell you the truth; ask them what they thought of the training and your techniques and use that information to improve your own skills.

Employee Benefits

The actual wages you pay may be only part of your employees' total compensation. While many very small companies do not offer a formal benefits program, more and more business owners have recognized that benefits—particularly in the area of insurance—are extremely important when it comes to attracting and retaining quality employees in their business. In most parts of the country, the employment rate is higher than it's been in decades, which means competition for good people is stiff.

Typical benefit packages include group insurance (your employees may pay all or a portion of their premiums), paid holidays, and vacations. You can build employee loyalty by seeking additional benefits that may be somewhat unusual—and they don't have to cost much. For example, if you're in a retail location, talk to other store owners in your shopping center to see if they're interested in providing reciprocal employee discounts. You'll not only provide your own employees with a benefit, but you may get some new customers out of the arrangement.

The Legal Side of Employees

The federal government affords employees legal protection in several aspects. If you have employees, there are several things you need to know about. They include:

- *Workers' compensation.* A type of insurance, WC covers three components involving employees injured on the job, including medical bills and lost wages of the employee, liability coverage for the employer, and an optional component covering things like lawsuits arising from discrimination, harassment, etc. Check the most up-to-date state and federal regulations.

- *FICA withholding.* You are required to withhold a certain percentage of your employees' pay plus contribute a portion to FICA tax, which provides employees with retirement and disability benefits.

- *Unemployment taxes.* These are at both the state and federal level and provide wages for unemployed workers.

- *Sexual harassment and discrimination laws.* Federal and state governments require that employees expect a workplace free from sexual harassment and discrimination as a result of race, color, creed, and even age.

- *OSHA.* The federal Occupational Safety and Health Administration oversees the laws that govern workplace safety—be aware of things like slippery floors, chemical use, safe use of tools, and a hazard-free workplace.

- *Americans with Disabilities Act.* This law was passed in 1990 to ensure that disabled workers could find employment in companies that have over 15 employees if "reasonable accommodations" would allow the disabled worker to do the job.

These are the critical ones but this is really just the tip of the iceberg when it comes to workers rights and the rules governing employees. Make sure you engage a lawyer or advisor who can keep you in line with all the laws if you decide to have employees.

Equipping
Your Business

Certainly creativity is one of the most important pieces of "equipment" you'll need, but there are a number of more mundane machines that are essential to your operation. You don't need every single piece of equipment listed in this chapter to get started, but you should at least consider each one and decide

▲

how it works in relation to your own goals and growth strategy. (Refer to our handy equipment checklist on page 96 to help you get started.)

Basic Office Equipment

Many entrepreneurs find a trip to the local office supply store more exciting than any mall. It's easy to get carried away when you're surrounded with an abundance of clever gadgets, all designed to make your working life easier and more fun. But if, like most new business owners, you're starting on a budget, discipline yourself to get only what you need. Consider these primary basic items:

- *Computer and printer.* A computer can help you manage complex bookkeeping and inventory control tasks, maintain customer records, and produce marketing materials. Even though a computer is not necessary for actually assembling baskets, it's an extremely valuable management and marketing tool and an essential element for growing a strong and profitable business. Computers are being enhanced faster than we can imagine. As of this writing, a desktop computer with the last premium version of Microsoft Windows, 1GB RAM, 160GB hard drive, a color printer, all the latest fastest DSL and wireless connections, plus a 17-inch monitor is retailing for just under $200!

- *Software.* Think of software as your computer's "brains," the instructions that tell your computer how to accomplish the functions you need. There are a myriad of programs on the market that will handle your accounting, inventory, customer information management, and other administrative requirements.

  Software can be a significant investment, so do a careful analysis of your own needs, then study the market and examine a variety of products before making a final decision.

- *Photocopier.* The photocopier is a fixture of the modern office and can be very useful to even the smallest gift basket business. You can get a basic, low-end, no-frills personal copier for a couple hundred dollars in just about any office supply store. More elaborate models increase proportionately in price. If you

Beware!
Though integrated, multifunction devices—such as a copier/printer/ fax machine or a fax/telephone/ answering machine—may cost less to acquire and take up less space in your office, you risk losing all these functions simultaneously if the equipment fails. Also, consider your anticipated volume of use with the machine's efficiency rating and cost to operate and compare that with stand-alone machines before making a final decision.

anticipate a heavy volume, consider leasing.

- *Fax machine.* For most gift basket businesses, fax capability is essential. You can either add a fax card to your computer or buy a stand-alone machine. If you use your computer, it must be on to send or receive faxes, and the transmission may interrupt other work. For most businesses, a stand-alone machine on a dedicated telephone line is a wise investment. Expect to pay $100 to $250 for a fax machine.

- *Internet service.* While most computers will come equipped with everything you need to get online, you will need to obtain an internet service provider. Avoid "dial-up" service, which is almost a thing of the past

> ## Bright Idea
> Rather than purchasing mail-processing equipment and doing the work in-house, consider outsourcing all or part of the labor involved in preparing large mailings. Check under "mailing services" in the Yellow Pages. Consider using a sheltered workshop for tasks such as stuffing envelopes and affixing postage; you can do a good deed by providing work for people with disabilities and get your mail processed at an extremely competitive rate. Check with your local United Way office or other charitable organization for a referral.

anyway but is exceedingly slow and known to keep kicking you off for reasons beyond comprehension. Your cable television provider may be a source of internet service as well; if you are homebased, you probably will be able to get it reasonably priced along with your television service. Also, if you are homebased and have internet service coming into the house but not to your business area, consider getting a wireless router. Most laptop computers come with built-in wireless modems, but you may have to get an external link for a desktop. Then you can use the internet service anywhere in the house.

- *Postage scale.* Unless all of your mail is identical, a postage scale is a valuable investment. An accurate scale takes the guesswork out of postage and will quickly pay for itself. It's a good idea to weigh every piece of mail to eliminate the risk of items being returned for insufficient postage or overpaying when you are unsure of the weight. Light mailers—1 to 12 articles per day—will be adequately served by inexpensive mechanical postal scales, which typically range from $10 to $25. If you are averaging from 12 to 24 items per day, consider a digital scale, which is somewhat more expensive—generally from $50 to $200—but significantly more accurate than a mechanical unit. If you send more than 24 items per day or use priority or expedited services frequently, invest in an electronic computing scale that weighs the item and then calculates the rate via the carrier of your choice, making it easy for you to make comparisons. Programmable electronic scales range from $80 to $250.

- *Postage meter.* Postage meters allow you to pay for postage in advance and print the exact amount on the mailing piece when it is used. Many postage meters can print in increments of one-tenth of a cent, which can add up to big savings for bulk mail users. Meters also provide a "big company" professional image, are more convenient than stamps, and can save you money in a number of ways. Postage meters are leased, not sold, with rates at about $30 per month. They require a license, which is available from your local post office. Only five manufacturers are licensed by the U.S. Postal Service to manufacture and lease postage meters; your local post office can provide you with contact information, or look online at the USPS website. There you can also find out about online postage.

> ### Bright Idea
>
> Postage stamps come in a wide array of sizes, designs, and themes and can add an element of color, whimsy, and even thoughtfulness to your mail. Some mailers prefer stamps because they look more personal; others prefer metered mail because it looks more "corporate." Make your decision based on your own individual style and the image you want to create for your company.
>
> Suggestion: Use metered mail for invoices, statements, and other "official" business, and stamps for thank-you notes and similar marketing correspondence that could use an extra personal touch.

- *Paper shredder.* A response to both a growing concern for privacy and the need to recycle and conserve space in landfills, shredders are becoming increasingly common in both homes and offices. They allow you to efficiently destroy incoming unsolicited direct mail, as well as sensitive internal documents before they are discarded. Shredded paper can be compacted much tighter than paper tossed in a wastebasket, and it can also be used as packing material. Light-duty shredders start at about $25, and heavier-capacity shredders run from $150 to $500.

Chances are you have some equipment in your possession already that is readily adaptable to your new business. Use the "Checklist of Existing Resources" in Appendix C to help you determine what you already have on hand.

Telecommunications

The ability to communicate quickly with your customers and suppliers is essential to any business, but especially a gift basket business where customers often have last-minute needs. Advancing technology gives you a wide range of telecommunications options. Most telephone companies have created departments dedicated to small and homebased businesses; contact your local telephone service provider and ask to speak with someone who can review your needs and help you put together a service and equipment package that will work for you. Specific elements to keep in mind include:

- *Telephone.* Whether you are homebased or in a commercial location, a single voice telephone line should be adequate during the startup period. As you grow and your call volume increases, you'll add more lines.

  Your actual telephone itself can be a tremendous productivity tool, and most of the models on the market today are rich in features you will find useful. Such features include automatic redial, which redials the last number called at regular intervals until the call is completed; programmable memory for storing frequently called numbers; and a speaker phone for hands-free use. You may also want call forwarding, which allows you to forward calls to another number when you're not at your desk, and call waiting, which signals you that another call is coming in while you are on the phone. Even more useful these days is caller ID, which, provided your phone has the right display mechanism, displays the number and person who is calling when the phone rings. These services are typically available through your telephone company for a monthly fee.

  If you're going to be spending a great deal of time on the phone, perhaps doing marketing or handling customer service, consider a headset for comfort and efficiency. A decent quality one will cost close to $100 but the sound quality is worth it over the cheaper ones. A cordless phone lets you move around freely while talking, but you still have to have a hand free to hold the phone or get a kink in your neck perching it on your shoulder—and risk pushing the wrong button with your chin and hanging up on an important customer in the middle of an order! You'll pay $70 to $150 for a two-line speaker phone with a variety of standard features necessary for a business.

- *Answering machine/voice mail.* Because your business phone should never go unanswered, you need some sort of reliable answering device to take calls when you can't do it yourself. Whether you buy a phone system with a built-in answering machine, a separate answering machine (expect to pay $40 to $150 for one that is suitable to a business), or use voice-mail

> ## Dollar Stretcher
>
> Just about any type of business equipment can be purchased secondhand for a fraction of its original retail cost. Check the classified section of your local newspaper and ask new equipment dealers if they have trade-ins or repossessions for sale. Careful shopping for used items can save hundreds of dollars.

service provided through your telephone company (anywhere from $6 to $20 per month) is a choice you must make depending on your personal preferences, work style, and needs.

- *Cell phone.* Once considered a luxury, cell phones have become standard equipment for most business owners. Most have features similar to your office phone—such as caller ID, call waiting, and voice mail—and equipment and services packages are very reasonably priced.

- *Pager.* A pager lets you know that someone is trying to reach you and lets you choose when you want to return the call. Many people use pagers in conjunction with cellular phones to conserve the cost of airtime. As with cellular phones, the pager industry is very competitive, so shop around for the best deal.

- *Toll-free number.* If you are targeting a customer base outside your local calling area, you'll want to provide them with a toll-free number so they can reach you without having to make a long-distance call. Most long-distance service providers offer toll-free numbers and have a wide range of service and price packages. Shop around to find the best deal for you. This can be a significant monthly expense, but it is known to pay for itself in sales.

- *E-mail.* Electronic mail is a now standard element in a company's communications package. It allows for fast, efficient, 24-hour communication. If you have e-mail, and you should, check your messages regularly and reply to them promptly.

Other Equipment

In addition to these basics, there are other items you may need, depending on your particular operation. They include:

- *Cash register.* For a retail operation, you need a way to track sales, collect money, and make change. You can do this with something as simple as a divided cash drawer and a printing calculator, or you can purchase a sophisticated, state-of-the-art point-of-sale system that is networked with your computer. Of course, the latter will cost somewhere between $1,200 and $5,000 per terminal and may not be a practical investment for a small startup operation. A preferable option is an electronic cash register (ECR), which can range from $600 to $3,000, and can be purchased outright, leased, or acquired under a lease-purchase agreement. The newer ECRs offer such options as payment records to designate whether a customer paid by cash, check, or charge; department price groupings (appropriate for stores with multiple departments so you can separate the prices for items in each department); sign-in keys to help you monitor cashiers and clerks; and product price groups (which let you organize products as they are rung up) for tracking inventory more effectively.

- *Credit and debit card processing equipment.* This could range from a simple imprint machine to an online terminal. Credit and debit card service providers are widely available, so shop around to understand the service options, fees, and equipment costs. Expect to pay about $500 for a "swipe" machine that reads the magnetic strip on cards. You'll also pay a transaction charge, which might be a flat rate (perhaps 20 to 30 cents) per transaction or a percentage (typically 1.6 to 3.5 percent) of the sale. You'll probably pay higher transaction fees for internet sales, because the fraud risk the bank is accepting is higher than with face-to-face transactions.

Basket-Assembling Equipment

The essential equipment required to assemble gift baskets is actually minimal. As your business grows, you may opt for more elaborate, sophisticated gadgets. But you can get started with just a work table (about 3 feet by 8 feet), heavy-duty scissors, a 120-inch measuring tape (to measure cellophane), tape dispensers with heavy bases, staplers, and a glue gun. If more than one person will be assembling baskets at the same time, you'll need separate workstations, each equipped with the essentials.

You don't have to spend a lot of money on your basic tools. For example, for less than $2, you can get an adequate cold glue gun that will seal decorative wrapping and hold items together and in place in the basket—but even hot glue guns are not expensive, typically ranging from $10 to $25.

Most gift basket makers wrap their baskets to secure the contents, either with cellophane or shrink wrap. Some basketeers think shrink wrap looks "tacky" and will only use cellophane; others use shrink wrap when shipping and cellophane when hand delivering; still others use shrink wrap on all their baskets. The

Dollar Stretcher

Most shrink-wrap packaging manufacturers offer equipment and supply combinations that can save you money over buying each individual piece separately. Be sure to ask about these deals before making a final purchase decision.

final decision is yours. To wrap a basket in cellophane, all you need is the cellophane, a pair of good scissors, and wire or ribbon to tie the cellophane. Shrink-wrapping systems vary tremendously in cost and complexity; your choices of equipment to shrink wrap or bag your baskets include:

- *Shrink-wrap system.* This device wraps your baskets quickly and professionally in clear or colored plastic films, sealing in the products that fill each basket. There is a wide range of shrink-wrap products on the market. You can purchase rolls of plastic film that you seal with a heat gun, or invest in a table machine with heat pads, dispensers, and sealing blocks. Expect to pay from $300 to $500 (or more) for a shrink-wrap system.

- *Heat gun.* This looks like an industrial-strength hairdryer—but don't use it on your hair. It is used to apply heat to wrapping film so it will shrink and provide a tight, securely wrapped basket. Expect to pay from $50 to $100 for a quality heat gun.

- *Heat sealers.* These sealing devices come in a variety of designs, and are used to seal shrink bags. Many will also seal Mylar balloons. Depending on style and purpose, sealers commonly range from $60 to $600—although you can spend as much as $3,000.

Equipment Checklist

Use the following checklist as a shopping guide to get your work space and store (if you start a retail operation) set up. Each item listed is not necessarily required before you start, but if you don't buy them now, you'll want to have them eventually.

Specialty Equipment
- ❑ Work space fixtures _____
- ❑ Work table(s) _____
- ❑ Crafting tools _____
- ❑ Heavy-duty scissors _____
- ❑ 120-inch measuring tape _____
- ❑ Glue gun _____
- ❑ Tape dispensers _____
- ❑ Shrink wrapper _____
- ❑ Heat gun _____
- ❑ Company vehicle _____
- ❑ Signage _____
- ❑ Security system _____
- ❑ Storage fixtures and hardware _____
- ❑ Storage shelves, cabinets _____

Store Equipment/Fixtures (for retail operations)
- ❑ Special displays and related hardware _____
- ❑ Display shelving _____
- ❑ Cash register _____
- ❑ Counter _____
- ❑ Marking guns _____
- ❑ Floor gondolas _____
- ❑ Pegboard (5 to 10 panels) _____

Equipment Checklist, continued

- ❑ Hooks _____
- ❑ Showcases (1 or 2) _____
- ❑ Wall gondolas (5 to 10) _____

Packaging/Shipping Equipment
- ❑ Hand truck _____
- ❑ High-speed tape dispenser _____
- ❑ Carton stapler _____
- ❑ Electronic scale _____
- ❑ Paper shredder _____

Office Furniture, Equipment, and Supplies
- ❑ Computer system (including printer) _____
- ❑ Typewriter _____
- ❑ Fax machine _____
- ❑ Software _____
- ❑ Phone system _____
- ❑ Answering machine or voice mail _____
- ❑ Uninterruptible power supply _____
- ❑ Zip drive backup _____
- ❑ Surge protector _____
- ❑ Calculator _____
- ❑ Copier _____
- ❑ Desk _____
- ❑ Desk chair _____
- ❑ Printer stand _____
- ❑ File cabinet(s) _____
- ❑ Bookcase _____
- ❑ Computer/copier paper _____
- ❑ Business cards _____
- ❑ Letterhead paper _____
- ❑ Matching envelopes _____
- ❑ Address stamp or stickers _____
- ❑ Extra printer cartridge _____
- ❑ Extra fax cartridge _____
- ❑ Zip drive disks _____
- ❑ Mouse pad _____
- ❑ Miscellaneous office supplies _____

Total Office Equipment and Furniture Expenditures _____

Inventory

Your initial inventory should be focused on baskets and other containers and the items that will go in them. As your business grows, you can expand your inventory to include other specialty gifts, such as local arts and crafts, personalized linen, jewelry, etc.

We've included a short list of suppliers in Appendix A to get you started with finding sources, and we've also provided an inventory checklist on page 103 to help you assemble your initial inventory. Many more suppliers advertise in various trade publications. You may even find them listed in your local Yellow Pages under "wholesalers."

Your inventory will consist of items you buy at both wholesale and retail prices. Wholesale purchases will include items and supplies you use in large quantities, for your most popular basket arrangements and as filler items. Retail purchases will typically consist of the merchandise you accumulate when you go shopping for customized basket materials. You'll keep certain basic items on hand all the time—the things you know you'll use over and over, like popular gourmet foods, candy, specialty coffees and teas, mugs, scented candles, and so on. The rest of your inventory will be different each month—sometimes even each week—depending on the season and the kinds of baskets you create.

Food for Thought

The Food and Drug Administration (FDA) requires that food items be properly labeled with ingredients and nutritional information. Products purchased from wholesale manufacturers should already be prepackaged and appropriately labeled. Certain food items, such as fresh fruit, are exempt from labeling requirements; most basketeers just buy those items as needed from local grocery stores. Be sure all food items are stored safely at appropriate temperatures, and check expiration dates regularly.

Your local health department can answer any questions you have about food product handling or direct you to an appropriate information source.

To sell alcohol, you must have a license issued by your state. In most states, liquor licenses are expensive and sometimes hard to obtain. A better strategy is to simply not provide alcohol; if your customers want an alcoholic beverage included in a basket, they may provide it themselves. Do not purchase it for them; that puts you in the position of selling liquor without a license, which is a serious crime.

Sample: Cost of Goods Sold—Merchandiser

(a) Cost of Goods Sold (Merchandiser)

For Period Ending December 31, 2002		Totals
Net Sales		$155,000
Beginning inventory, January 1, 2002	$29,367	
Merchandise purchases	$74,190	
Freight	$4,637	
Cost of Goods Available for Sale		$108,194
Less ending inventory, December 31, 2002	$30,913	
Cost of Goods Sold		$77,281

(b) Cost of Goods Manufactured

For Period Ending December 31, 2002	Totals	
Work in process inventory, January 1, 2002	$2,318	
Inventory, January 1, 2002	$20,866	
Purchases	$35,549	
Freight in	$1,545	
Cost of Materials Available for Use		$57,960
Less inventory, December 31, 2002	$22,412	
Cost of Materials Used		$35,548
Direct Labor		$20,093
Indirect labor	$3,091	
Factory utilities	$12,365	
Factory supplies used	$3,091	
Insurance & taxes	$773	
Depreciation	$4,637	
Total Manufacturing Overhead		$23,957
Total Manufacturing Costs		$79,598
Total Work in Process During Period		$81,916
Less work in process inventory, December 31, 2002	$4,635	
Cost of Goods Manufactured		$77,281

For a gift basket business, shopping is a major behind-the-scenes activity. Depending on your volume, expect shopping and ordering to take anywhere from one to four hours a day on average.

Successful gift basket business owners are industrious shoppers, constantly searching for bargains and new supply sources. Some of their shopping tips include:

- Attend local, state, and national gift shows as often as possible but at least twice a year. Show calendars are published in various trade magazines and on the internet (see Appendix A for a listing of industry publications).

- Have suppliers put you on their mailing lists to help you stay abreast of sales and other money-saving announcements.

- Buy in bulk to take advantage of quantity discounts.

- Look for suppliers with diversified product lines, flexible terms, and small minimum-purchase requirements.

- Don't overlook local merchants; many will offer prices and terms competitive with national companies and will have a bond with you as a fellow community vendor.

From the very beginning, make it a point to build strong relationships with your suppliers—they'll be an invaluable source of information on purchasing. Use their expertise and seriously consider their recommendations when it comes to ordering the proper types and amounts of baskets and other inventory items. Suppliers have a vested interest in your long-term success, because the more you sell, the more you'll buy from them.

Let's take a look at your inventory categories:

- *Baskets.* Don't be confined by the technical definition of basket, because in your business, a "basket" may be anything from a traditional container made of woven wood strips to a plastic pail, ceramic pot, or even a football helmet. Even so, you're likely to order most of your baskets from a large wholesale supplier. Stick to a few types of baskets at first, such as long-handled Easter-type baskets, planters, fruit bowls, and small picnic hampers. You can expand your selection later as business increases. In the meantime, if you need a special basket, you can always buy it at its retail price and mark up the cost.

Smart Tip

Tip...

When Dana S. was starting up her business, Gift Baskets by Your Design in New Hampshire, she found out about a woman who was shutting down her gift basket business. "I bought out [her] inventory," Dana says. "For $1,200 I bought thousands of dollars of inventory."

Take advantage of these opportunities if you can; just be careful that you are buying inventory that isn't dated (especially food items) and that you can actually use in the kind of baskets you plan to create.

- *Contents.* You need to decide on your product line before you begin shopping for the items you'll put in your baskets. Even though you will custom-make each basket, many of the items will be the same and can be purchased in bulk.

  Make a list of the items and quantities that will be included in your standard baskets and order enough merchandise to fill at least 20 to 30 baskets of each type—more if you can afford it. Remember, you will pay less per item for larger quantities; just be sure the items you order in large quantities are items you'll use.

Beware!
As you begin building your inventory, it's easy to get excited about the various types of merchandise you can buy and then start making impulse purchases. The problem with this approach is that you'll end up with pretty baskets that contain clever items, but there won't be a focal point to them. Baskets need a focus and should be geared to the recipient.

For example, if you have a coffee basket as one of your standards, make a list of how much coffee (regular, decaffeinated, flavored), related snacks, mugs, etc., you'll need to assemble 20 or 30 of these baskets. If you also offer a personal-care basket, your list will include lotion, bath oil, bubble bath, scented soaps, fancy sponges, and so on.

The one-of-a-kind items you'll need for special baskets that don't match the products on your standard list will be purchased individually and only as you need them. For example, someone may order a custom basket for a favorite nephew who has passed his bar exam and landed a job with a prestigious law firm, or a niece who has opened her own medical practice. These are unique situations and mean you'll have to shop retail to get the most appropriate items. However, many retailers will sell to you at wholesale, or at least a discount off retail, if you let them know you are buying the merchandise to resell and show them your sales tax permit (also called a reseller or seller's permit). This permit also allows you to avoid paying sales tax on merchandise at the time you purchase it.

If you like to shop, this part of your business will be fun. You can use all your creativity to come up with items that fit the guidelines your customers give you.

- *Decorative and packaging inventory.* This category includes all the decorations, trimmings, stuffing labels, wrapping, and cards that you use in your baskets. Most of these items are available in bulk and include ribbon, bows (paper and fabric), plastic grass, excelsior straw, tissue paper, shredded iridescent and Mylar paper, blank miniature cards with envelopes, tape, tassels, doilies, etc.

  Cellophane is a must because it can be both functional and decorative. Because it wraps the basket to help secure the contents, it can also add an element of style. Get at least one roll of 40 inches by 100 feet clear cellophane and,

Trade Show Tips

Attending trade shows and conferences with large exhibit halls can be a lot of work! Here are some trade-show tips to help you look forward to trade shows:

○ *Wear comfortable shoes.* I'll repeat that: Wear comfortable shoes. This is perhaps the most important tip you can get. Although these days it is possible to combine style with comfort, if you can't get both, go for the comfort. Unless you choose to wear bright red stilettos, no one will notice your shoes except you when your feet start killing you and you can't wait for the day to end. Comfortable shoes allow you to concentrate on the bargains, not your feet.

○ *Use discretion when picking up catalogs.* If you are just looking to remember a certain supplier, take a business card or other small item with their name on it and look them up online later. Tote around only those catalogs you really think you will use later—your back and shoulder will thank you for it.

○ *Don't allow yourself to be wowed by the moment.* You don't want to place orders that you will regret when you get home. Is something really a bargain if you don't actually need it? Or need that many of it?

○ *Make out a budget and bring it along.* If you have a written budget to refer to, you can look at it when you are considering a purchase. And stop once in a while and deduct the purchases you have made from your budget so you know where you stand.

○ *Attend seminars and workshops.* These are great learning experiences as well as a good chance to meet new people—and to sit down for a while! Many conferences offer lots of workshops that cost no more than the general price of admission. You may be surprised at what ideas you come home with—and with some renewed enthusiasm!

if you have the cash, a second roll of red. The colored cellophane is an easy way to add brilliance and interest to a plain wicker basket.

If you ship your baskets, you'll also need packaging materials, which include boxes of various sizes, fill material (bubble wrap, packing popcorn, or shredded newspaper), packing tape, and mailing labels.

- *Office supplies.* This includes your business stationery, business cards, invoices, and other printed materials, as well as file folders, note pads, paper clips, staples, and other miscellaneous operations materials. While this is not a major expense for most businesses, you should still make these purchases thoughtfully. Office supply superstores and warehouse clubs are excellent sources for office supplies at competitive prices.

- *Special purchases.* As you shop for your regular and custom inventory items, you may occasionally run across a special deal on goods that's worth taking advantage of, even though you may not have a specific use in mind for them when you buy them. For example, Chris K. recalls finding a large supply of sterling silver piggy banks for $3 each in a small import store. When she bought them and started including them in baskets, she found them to be extremely popular, even to the point of creating a sense of urgency among customers who wanted them before the supply ran out.

This style of purchasing is essentially impulse buying, and it's not a bad practice as long as your tastes coincide with your patrons'. It's a good idea to delay making these kinds of speculative special purchases until you've been in business a while and have established a clientele you know well.

Inventory Checklist

No two gift basket businesses carry identical inventory. What and how much you stock will depend on the size of your operation and your customers' preferences. Use this checklist as a starting point for developing your individual inventory of supplies and gift items.

Gift Basket Supplies
- ❏ Baskets/containers
- ❏ Packing materials
- ❏ Decorative materials
- ❏ Shrink-wrap film and/or cellophane
- ❏ Products/gifts

Retail Supplies
- ❏ Cash register tape
- ❏ Shopping bags
- ❏ Gift boxes
- ❏ Sales tags and/or labels

Packaging/Shipping Supplies
- ❏ Sealing tape
- ❏ Boxes
- ❏ Mailing labels
- ❏ Cushioned mailers
- ❏ Packing materials

Paper Chase

A great source of free shredded paper is your local post office. "I wrote a letter to my local postmaster and asked him for his shredded nonsensitive returned mail to use as stuffer for the bottom of my baskets," Yvette L. says. "I got more than I could handle." She lined her baskets with tissue paper, filled them with the shredded mail, then added another layer of tissue. The result was attractive, colorful, and elegant—and extremely inexpensive. Another source of inexpensive paper filler is the end rolls of newsprint that are available from your local newspaper; often these are free or available for a nominal charge.

Inventory Control

There is much more to managing inventory than simply shopping. You have to know what to buy, when to buy it, and how much you need. Buy the wrong items and they'll sit on your shelf forever and never make a profit for you. Buy at the wrong time and you may not have things in stock when you need them. Buy too little and you won't have enough to meet your customers' demands. Buy too much and you'll tie up your capital unnecessarily. Certainly a crystal ball would make purchasing much easier, but even without one, you can develop an inventory control system that works. Whether you use a manual or computer method, you'll need to consider several issues.

Basic Stock

Your basic stock must fulfill two functions: First, it should provide customers with a reasonable assortment of products. Second, it should cover the normal sales demands of your business.

To calculate basic stock accurately, you must review actual sales during an appropriate time period, such as a full year of business. Since you will have no previous sales and stocking figures to guide you during startup, you must project your first year's sales based on your business plan.

Lead Times

Lead time—the length of time between placing an order and receiving a product—is an important factor when calculating basic stock. For example, if you use approximately 15 Easter-style baskets per week and it takes three weeks from the time you place the order for the product to arrive, then you must reorder these items when your stock is down to about 45 baskets. If you wait until you run out of baskets to reorder, you'll lose sales—and customers.

It's also a good idea to incorporate a safety margin into your basic inventory figures to protect against external factors that can contribute to delays. You will get better at determining the right safety margin after you have been in business a while and have some direct experience to build on.

> **Smart Tip**
>
> Avoid using old, wadded newspaper or paper bags as filler. It's tacky, it looks cheap, and when people take the baskets apart, you don't want yours to look like it was prepared by an amateur.

Excess Inventory

Excess inventory creates extra overhead, and that costs you money. Inventory that sits in your storeroom does not generate sales or profits—it shrinks your bottom line. Losses caused by excess inventory come in the form of:

- Debt service on loans to purchase the excess inventory
- Additional personal property tax on unsold inventory
- Increased insurance costs on the greater value of the inventory in stock

A common and natural reaction to excess inventory is to reduce the price and sell it quickly. While this may solve your overstocking problem, it also reduces your return on investment. All your financial projections assume that you will receive the full retail price for your goods. If you overstock and reduce your prices by 15 percent to 25 percent to jettison the excess inventory, you'll lose money you had counted on in budgeting.

You may be tempted to respond to the excess inventory issue with overly cautious reordering. But doing this risks creating a shortage in stock, and the result could be a drop in sales. The solution is to plan well to avoid accumulating excess inventory, establish a realistic safety margin, and order only what you're sure you can sell. And you might be able to get some items at big box/warehouse stores as cheaply as wholesale plus shipping.

Tracking Inventory

A critical part of managing inventory is tracking it—that means knowing what you have on hand, what's on order and when it will arrive, and what you've already sold. This information allows you to plan your purchases intelligently, quickly recognize fast-moving items that need to be reordered, and identify slow-moving merchandise that should be marked down and moved out.

There are a variety of inventory-tracking methods you can use, from basic hand-written records to computerized bar code systems. The gift basket business owners we talked to use simple systems, most on basic computer databases. Your accountant can help you develop a system that will work for your particular situation.

Vehicles

The largest single piece of equipment you'll need is a vehicle to make local basket deliveries, take packages going out of the area to shipping companies such as UPS, and for shopping expeditions. You need a reliable, fuel-efficient vehicle with sufficient cargo capacity. Some basketeers drive vans; others have found that smaller cars with fold-down backseats and hatchbacks are sufficient and easier to maneuver in heavy traffic.

If the vehicle you presently own is suitable, using it—at least during the startup process—will conserve your initial capital outlay. If it's not, or if you prefer to maintain a personal vehicle and a business vehicle, you'll have to lease or purchase one that will meet your needs.

When looking for a vehicle, keep in mind what you are going to be using it for. For instance, if you decide on a minivan, be sure to buy one whose seats are easily removed to make room for boxes headed out to be shipped. But you also want the seats to be easy to reinstall if you decide to sell the vehicle. There are many vehicles on the market that are designed especially to carry cargo, with open areas in the back, square corners to make transporting square boxes easier, and doors that open widely or a wide back door that allows you to put boxes in and take them out with ease.

Unless your projections are for huge sales that require lots of space, get as energy-efficient a vehicle as you can. As of this writing, gas prices have gone through the roof and are unlikely to come down to any levels we have seen in the past. If you will have need to move only the occasional large shipment, get the energy-efficient vehicle and rent a large box truck when you need it. It is probably going to be much cheaper that way.

No matter what you buy, be meticulous in maintaining the vehicle with regular oil changes and making repairs when they arise. A vehicle can be a major asset for a gift basket company; if you decide to close the business it can be sold. Or even if you have a major cash crunch, you can sell your vehicle and use your personal vehicle or rent one for a while. But if you want to sell the vehicle for what it's worth, it should be well maintained.

Security

Whether you are homebased or in a retail location, remember that small merchandise, office equipment, and cash attract burglars, robbers, and shoplifters. Not only do you need to protect your inventory and equipment with alarms, lighting, and a careful selection of employees, but you also need to secure your personal safety as well as that of your employees.

Begin by investigating your area's crime history to determine what kind of measures you need to take. To learn whether your proposed or existing location has a high crime rate, check with the local police department's community relations department or crime prevention officer. Most will gladly provide free information on safeguarding your business and will often even personally visit your site to discuss specific crime prevention strategies. Many also offer training seminars for small retailers and their employees on workplace safety and crime prevention.

Common techniques merchants use to enhance security and reduce shoplifting include mirrors, alarms, and video monitors. Technology is bringing the cost of these items down rapidly, and installing them may also earn you discounts on your insurance. You can also increase the effectiveness of your security system by discreetly posting signs in your store windows and around the store announcing the presence of the equipment.

Marketing
Your Business

Marketing is something many people don't like to do, but it can be as creative and as much fun as actually making the baskets. And no matter how clever and attractive your baskets are, if no one knows they exist they won't sell all by themselves—you need to market them. Don't be discouraged if your marketing efforts don't produce an immediate response. Especially when you're marketing to businesses, you will find it's common to present your products to a corporate buyer, then wait months before they call you.

Plan to expand the marketing section of your business plan into an overall marketing plan. There are issues and ideas specific to the gift basket business that you need to know as you develop your plan. For example, one of your biggest marketing challenges will involve educating your customers to the fact that they can call on you at the last minute. Many people still believe baskets are gifts that must be planned well in advance; they're inclined to turn to florists for a last-minute, oops-I-forgot type of gift.

We asked successful gift basket business owners what specific techniques work for them, and here's what they said.

The Marketing Plan

You did a business plan and your business plan included a section on marketing. But if you want to have enough customers to succeed and eventually grow your business, you should develop a separate marketing plan.

A marketing plan will allow you to:
- Chart growth in the gift industry
- Define the market you serve
- Define your customers
- Determine the strengths and weaknesses of the competition
- Project sales
- Establish strategies to achieve your marketing goals
- Establish a market niche

That's a lot of important stuff!

Your marketing plan should consist of:
- An executive summary about yourself and any key personnel
- A description of your gift baskets
- Goals and objectives
- A market analysis
- Description of your customers
- Analysis of your business's competition
- Marketing tactics
- Financial projections
- A summary

Plan to use a combination of straight narrative as well as a chart or two. Most of the latest office software includes the ability to automatically make a pie chart or graph out of a spreadsheet. This isn't just for looks, but allows you a more dramatic way of looking at a collection of numbers. Seeing the figures showing your customers as 17 percent in their 20s, 20 percent in their 30s, and 63 percent over 40 looks pretty impressive when you see a big old chunk of the pie chart devoted to the over-40 customer.

Make Customer Service a Marketing Tool

There is probably no business where customer service works better as a marketing tool than in gift baskets. You'll have a lot of opportunity to interact with your customers; take advantage of each contact to demonstrate your superior service. Then take it a step further. For example, Sue C. sends handwritten thank-you notes to new customers, customers she hasn't heard from in a while, and customers who place special orders. Each customer gets two or three notes a year. She could do them on her word processor, but she believes the personal touch of being handwritten makes a difference in how they are received.

Get Lost

If you're making deliveries to an area with many potential customers, such as an office building or small office park, take the time to get lost. Sue C. never makes a delivery without carrying a handful of brochures and business cards because people in elevators, hallways, and even on the street will stop and comment on the basket she's carrying—and her response includes giving them a card and a brochure.

When she has time, she will deliberately get "lost" in a building. "Sometimes I parade a basket up and down every floor," Sue says. "I need people to see it. It's too funny when a man comes up and says, 'Oh, is that for me?'—especially when it's bubble bath and potpourri. But the guy wants it! I enjoy seeing and meeting people. I talk and I sell and I hand people my business card—I've gotten a number of customers that way."

Give Baskets Away

Your most effective advertising is your product itself. When you meet someone with the potential to become a good customer, send

> **Tip...**
>
> **Smart Tip**
> Ask every new customer how he or she found out about your business. Make a note of where they heard about you and what kind of business they represent. This will let you know how well your various marketing efforts are working. You can then decide to increase certain programs and eliminate those that either aren't working or are attracting a type of business you don't want.

them a complimentary basket with your brochure and several business cards. Once they see what you do, they'll call you when they need to send a gift.

Once a customer is on board, send them an occasional basket as a gesture of appreciation for their business. Be sure the basket is designed to make them think about another opportunity for buying a basket.

Reward Referrals

Rewarding customer referrals can be a smart investment—one that builds client relations and encourages future referrals. An existing customer who refers a new customer to Christine M. gets 10 percent off their next order.

Claire S. takes a different approach to referrals. She has a stock of cute teddy bears, and each time anyone makes a referral, she donates one of those bears to a sick child through the Make-a-Wish Foundation in the referring person's name. It's a way to let existing customers know how much she appreciates their confidence and give back to the community at the same time.

Bright Idea

Gift baskets are a great way for your customers to showcase gift items they've already purchased. Let them know that when they have an heirloom, photograph, piece of art, or other special item, you can make it the centerpiece of a custom gift basket.

An important point to keep in mind about referrals is that people rarely make a referral because you're going to give them something. They make referrals because they like what you do, they believe you'll do a good job for the other person, and when you do, you make them look like stars because they were smart enough to know you. But a referral reward of some sort is a way to emphasize to your existing customers how important referrals are to you.

Cold Call

Christine M. periodically schedules a day to make cold calls in industrial parks or office buildings. She takes a brochure, her business card, and any pertinent seasonal information and visits as many businesses as she can. It's tiring, she admits, but worth it—and far more effective doing it in person than on the phone.

Don't let limited resources stop you from getting out there. You only need one nice suit or dress and one sample basket. It's great if you can afford to leave a sample behind, but that's not essential—the main thing is to show prospective customers what you can do. But if you use the same sample basket over and over, be sure to rewrap it every few days to keep it looking fresh.

Dear Customer

Marketing to basket recipients lets you provide superior customer service while developing new business at the same time. Here's a sample letter to send out a few days after delivering a basket. Be sure each letter is personally addressed and signed.

Dear [insert the recipient's name]:

Recently, we delivered a gift basket to you from [insert customer/ sender's name].

We are very proud of the reputation we've established in the community, and we are committed to providing the highest-quality products and service. We hope you were pleased with your basket. If for any reason you were not totally delighted, would you please take a moment to call and let us know?

We offer a wide range of standard and custom gift baskets for all occasions and within all budgets. If we can ever be of assistance with your gift-giving needs, please let us know.

Sincerely,

[Your name]

Market to Basket Recipients

The recipients of your gift baskets are a great source of potential new customers. They've seen your work and know your quality and service. Be sure they know how to reach you when they need to send a gift.

Your company name and telephone number should be in or on every basket you prepare at least three times. Put one business

Bright Idea
Use special purchases as a marketing tool. When you find a deal on a clever gift item or an unusual basket, let your customers know what you've got and that they need to buy now to take advantage of this special purchase.

Bright Idea

If you have a regular corporate customer, consider ordering printed labels with their name as well as yours to put on the baskets. Labels are not expensive, and it's a great relationship builder when your customer knows the baskets you send will have a professional label that says "Compliments of XYZ Co., prepared by The Basket Maker." The label should also include your contact information. If the basket is for a specific holiday, such as Christmas, consider including an appropriate seasonal message. It's a small investment that can pay off big.

card on the bottom of the basket before you line and stuff it; next, nestle another card among the contents so it's not visible when the basket is finished, but will be there when the basket is opened; then, once the basket it wrapped, attach another card or sticker to the outside. Most people either ignore or lose the outside sticker because they're excited about opening the basket, but the cards inside let them know how to find you if they want to order from you.

Christine M. has turned following up with recipients into both a marketing and customer service tool. Every recipient of a basket receives a follow-up letter that mentions the name of the sender, stresses the company's commitment to quality and service, asks if the basket was satisfactory, and includes a business card and an invitation to call if the recipient ever needs to send a basket. Customers appreciate the letter because it puts their name in front of the recipient an extra time, recipients are impressed by the follow-up, and Christine has an opportunity to acquire a new customer. (See "Dear Customer" on page 113 for a sample letter you can use, or create your own.)

Claire S. does her follow-up by phone. "When you send out a gift, wait a day or two and call as a follow-up to make sure they received their gift and everything was acceptable and arrived in good condition," she advises. "You get all these wonderful reviews and you feel great."

Once you're confident the recipient has received and is happy with the basket, put them in your database so they receive your direct-mail pieces and will have the opportunity to buy from you in the future.

Make Yourself Visible

One of the simplest ways to build business and set yourself apart from the competition, says Christine M., is to just get out there and be visible. Knock on doors, hand out brochures, go to networking events—do whatever it takes to make sure people know about your company and understand what you do.

You must also stay visible with your existing clientele. Plenty of other gift providers would like their business, so you need to keep reminding them that you're the best game in town.

Target Lesser-Known Holidays

Help your customers find reasons to send gift baskets by promoting lesser-known holidays. When Yvette L. found out about Nurses' Day (which is May 6), she realized there were 12 major hospitals within an hour's drive of her business. She made a dozen $10 sample baskets for Nurses' Day and took one to each hospital in the area. She asked to see the person in charge of Nurses' Day—it varied by hospital; sometimes it was the marketing department, at other places it was administration or human resources—gave them the basket, and explained that it was just a suggestion and she could put together whatever they wanted. The entire effort cost her about $60 in supplies and less than a day of time, but within an hour of the first delivery, she had an order for 400 baskets. Another hospital didn't bother with the smaller baskets and instead ordered four $300 baskets.

More important, she had established a relationship with the hospitals. One set her up on a program to deliver a $25 basket to each doctor on his or her birthday; with 200 doctors on their permanent staff, that was a sizeable order. And the hospitals that bought Nurses' Day baskets came back for Doctors' Day.

Just about every occupation has a "day" to honor it. Hallmark publishes a calendar of the more common holidays and special events; some research in your library or on the internet will tell you about others. Also, *Chase's Calendar of Events* is published by McGraw-Hill, updated annually, and now comes with a CD-ROM; this book will give you great ideas for promotions tied to events.

Stat Fact

The top five best-selling occasions (besides holidays) for giving a gift basket, according to *Gift Basket Review*, are:

- ○ New baby
- ○ Birthdays
- ○ Thank you
- ○ Get well/cheer up
- ○ Funeral/sympathy

Advertising

Direct-mail advertising is an excellent tool for gift basket businesses. Sue C. created a database of people who have purchased from her and people who have been recipients of her baskets. She sends mailers before every holiday.

Christine M. sends a postcard to her entire database at the beginning of every month. If there's a holiday during that month, the card focuses on gift ideas for that holiday. If it's a no-holiday month, the card might focus on birthdays or an area of her business that's been slow. Occasionally, she'll send out an extra card. For example, in April, she sends a general card to her entire database, then another card to her corporate accounts reminding them of Secretaries' Day, which is the fourth Wednesday

Stat Fact

According to *Gift Basket Review* magazine, the preferred types of advertising among established gift basket businesses are networking/word-of-mouth; telephone directory (Yellow Pages listing); direct mail; brochures; and newspaper advertising.

of that month. She notes that an interesting result of direct mail is that business will increase with each mailing, regardless of the card's topic because it reminds people about her business in general. For example, she might have sent a card about birthday baskets that made the customer think about sending a get-well basket.

Yellow Page ads can generate a significant number of calls, but they are expensive, especially for a very small operation. Calculate how many baskets you'll need to sell to cover the cost of the ad and then decide if you can—and want to—handle that volume.

Most ads in other types of directories—neighborhood specialty directories, statewide consumer directories, even women-owned business directories, etc.—rarely generate enough business to justify their cost. If you're considering an ad in one of those books, call several advertisers in businesses similar to yours and find out how much business they get from the ad.

Look in Appendix C at the "Market Planning Checklist" to help you plan a marketing campaign.

Trade Shows

In addition to attending trade shows to find merchandise and learn more about running your business, consider exhibiting in trade shows to market your products. Local trade shows can provide a tremendous amount of exposure at a very affordable cost.

There are two types of shows—consumer (which focus on home, garden, and other consumer themes) and business-to-business (where exhibitors market their products and services to other companies). Both can work for a gift basket business.

"When you go to a show, you're tapping into an audience that is typically outside your network," says trade-show consultant Allen Konopacki. "The other important thing is that the individuals who are going to shows are usually driven by a need. In fact, 76 percent of the people who go to a show are looking to make some kind of a decision on a purchase in the near future."

To find out about local shows in your area, call your local chamber of commerce or convention center and ask for a calendar. You can also check out *Trade Show Week Show Directory*, which should be available in your public library, or do an internet search.

Trade-Show Exhibit Do's and Don'ts

A carnival-like atmosphere permeates many trade shows. Certainly you want everyone involved to enjoy themselves, but remember—this is a business occasion. Your booth is your store/office for the duration of the show, and it should be a place where you are proud to meet with customers. Establishing dress and conduct rules for your booth ahead of time will make your trade-show experience much more rewarding.

○ *No smoking, drinking, eating, or gum chewing by booth staffers.* Most exhibit halls no longer allow smoking in the building anyway. While most shows provide refreshments, bringing food and beverages into the booth creates an unattractive mess. Who wants to talk to a sales rep whose mouth is full?

○ *Dress appropriately.* Just because the show is taking place in a resort doesn't mean you should wear shorts. Standard business attire and comfortable shoes are your best bet.

○ *Staff the booth properly.* Two people for every 10 feet of space is a good rule of thumb. The key is to make sure your booth is not overcrowded with your own people, or understaffed so visitors cannot get the assistance they need.

○ *Take regular breaks.* Trade shows can be exhausting. Plan to allow everyone a few minutes away from the booth at scheduled intervals. Also allow time for personnel to see the entire show as early as possible; they'll gain a feel for the competition and pick up ideas for your next show.

○ *Remain standing and talk to each other only when necessary.* Visitors may be reluctant to approach your booth if it appears your salespeople are just relaxing and having a great time chatting among themselves.

When you have identified potential shows, contact the sponsor for details. Find out who will attend—show sponsors should be able to estimate the total number and give you demographics so you can tell if the attendees fit your target-market profile. Also ask if it's appropriate to make sales from your booth so you can plan your display and bring sufficient inventory.

Give as much thought to the setup of your booth as you would to an in-store display. Your exhibit does not need to be elaborate or expensive, but it does need to be professional and inviting. Avoid trying to cram so much into your booth that it looks cluttered. Your signage should focus first on the problems you solve for clients, then list your company name. Even though the show sponsors will probably provide one, do not put a table across the front of your exhibit space; that creates a visual and psychological barrier and will discourage visitors from coming in.

Don't leave your booth unattended during exhibit hours. First, it's a security risk—in a busy show, it would be easy for someone to walk off with valuable merchandise. But more important, you could miss a tremendous sales opportunity. Even if you're a one-person operation, find someone who can work the show with you so you can take breaks during the day.

Consider some sort of giveaway item such as pens, mugs, or notepads imprinted with your company name. But, says Konopacki, do not display these items openly; that will only crowd your booth with "trade show tourists." Instead, store them discreetly out of sight, and

Smart Tip

Tip...

Trade shows and conventions are valuable business tools, whether you're attending to shop and learn or exhibiting to get more business. For more information on how to get more out of trade shows and to find show schedules, visit these trade-show websites: Incomm Research Center, tradeshow research.com; Trade Show Central, tscentral.com; Trade Show News Network, tsnn .com; and Tradeshow Week On-Line, tradeshowweek.com.

Show Potential

When exhibiting at trade shows, keep in mind that the other exhibitors are potential customers for you. Yvette L.'s largest single customer was a soft drink manufacturer she met at a local business-to-business trade show sponsored by the Oklahoma Small Business Development Center. They occupied adjacent booths. After her booth was set up, but before the exhibit hall opened, she introduced herself to the company's regional director. Before the show was over, she had a $6,000 order—baskets to be sent to the spouses of the members of the company's sales team to thank them for their patience while the company reached a tough sales goal.

"They ordered these huge $50 picnic baskets and said whatever I wanted to do was fine—they would just judge by my work whether or not they would use me again," Yvette says. Apparently they liked what she did, because from then on, they placed similar-sized orders at least four times a year, and in between ordered baskets for Secretaries' Day, Bosses' Day, birthdays, and employees who had new babies. Aside from the corporate orders, company employees also used her services for personal gifts.

present them individually as appropriate. You should also have a stock of brochures, business cards, and perhaps discount coupons.

To collect lead information for later follow-up, give away a gift basket. Hold a drawing that people must register for, and make the registration form a lead-qualification tool. For example, if it's a business-to-business show, the registration form should ask their name, company name, whether or not they ever buy corporate gifts, whom in their company should be contacted to learn more about what you have to offer, and, of course, complete address and telephone information. At a consumer show, find out how many gift baskets they typically buy in a year, and where they buy them, and get an address so you can put them on your mailing list if their potential warrants it. Depending on the size and duration of the show, consider giving away more than one basket so you can hold drawings several times during the course of the show.

When the show is over, immediately send a follow-up letter to all the qualified leads you collected, thanking them for visiting your booth and reminding them of the products and services you offer. Don't assume they'll keep the information they picked up at the show; chances are, it will be lost in the pile of material from other exhibitors.

Smart Tip

A simple merchandising strategy is to name your baskets. Give each standard design a name that is clever, easy to remember, and fits with the theme of the basket. "Pamper Thyself" is a good name for a basket of lotions and scented soaps; a basket of cooking utensils and gourmet foods could be called the "Kitchen Kollection"; and the "Bridal Basket" might contain a lace garter, small picture frames, and white linen handkerchiefs. Use these names in your brochures and as part of your retail display. Beside each displayed basket, put a placard with the name, contents, price, and a descriptive blurb that suggests how the basket can be used.

Stat Fact

The bestselling holidays for gift baskets after Christmas are Valentine's Day, Mother's Day, Secretaries' Day, Thanksgiving, Easter, and Jewish holidays.

Public Relations and Promotions

An easy way to promote your gift basket business is to give a few away. Call local radio stations that reach your target market and ask to speak to their promotions manager. Offer to give them one or several baskets to use as prizes for on-air contests and promotions. You can either give them actual baskets or coupons their listeners can redeem. Your company name and location will be announced several times on the air during the contest, providing you with valuable free exposure, and it's always possible that the winner will become a paying customer.

You can also donate baskets to be used as door prizes at professional meetings or for nonprofit organizations to use as raffle prizes. Just be sure every basket you give away is clearly identified as being donated by you and that your card is on the outside and at the bottom of the basket.

Be bold when giving baskets away. Yvette L. had a friend whose husband appeared on *The Oprah Winfrey Show* to discuss something that had nothing to do with gift baskets. Yvette made a huge Oklahoma gift basket, which her friend's husband hand delivered to Winfrey, who responded with a very gracious thank-you letter. That letter is framed and has become part of Yvette's marketing package.

Selling
in Cyberspace

Having a website is almost a must for any serious business these days. And with a business like gift baskets, it is imperative. Websites let people from all over the world see and buy your baskets at any time, day or night. Even people who live in the same town expect to be able to look on your website at what you offer and see if they are interested before making a trip to your retail site. It's just part of doing business in the 21st century.

If you aren't going to be web-based, for which having a website is clearly a must, then here are some things to consider in deciding that a website is important for your business:

- Websites give you the ability to change content quickly and cheaply, making it easy to keep the information you have out there up-to-date. Printing a brochure does not afford you that ease of change.
- Customers can readily get information, or more information, on your business just by looking at your website.
- The entire world is your market.
- You can track the results of your marketing efforts more easily with website "hits" and questions/orders you get from your site.
- You gift basket business is open 24/7/365.

Setting Up a Website

If you are one of those people who claim to be computer illiterate and are proud of it, get over it now if you are going into business. If you are adept at using a computer and want to design your own website, that's great. But be sure it is professional looking. Just like a physical retail shop, you need your website to express the kind of business you have. Look at the differences in any retail world. When a potential buyer walks into a Cadillac showroom, they expect to have a high-quality experience compared to what they would encounter if they were to be shopping at their everyday Ford dealership. Harley-Davidson motorcycle dealerships are spotless works of art; they know that their middle-aged customer base is almost completely different from, say, the young dirt bike buyer. Check out all the websites of different products you are familiar with and get a sense of how their site caters to their buyer base.

If you don't feel like you can create the right website, consider hiring a professional web design company. The cost is typically not out of reach; you can expect to spend at least $1,000 for a well-designed site. You will also incur monthly charges to have it "hosted"—someone with a large server keeps everything coming and going. Hosting fees (from as little as $30 a month to several hundred, depending on the complexity of your web business) usually include a certain amount of monthly changes.

Before you hire a designer, look at lots of other websites and make sure you can give the designer ideas on what you like and don't like in the websites you see.

Find web designers by searching online or noticing who designed the sites you like. The designer doesn't have to be local to design your site—everything can be done, well, online!

You can also buy "template" web designs—you fill the details into a basic design. Take a look at Chichester, New Hampshire-based Dana Sonia's Gift Baskets by Your Design website (nhgiftbaskets.com). There are many template companies to choose from, such as baskweb.com, dreamtemplate.com, and web.com. You don't have to be a computer programming wiz to use them, they are designed to be put together by anyone with basic computer skills.

But Sonia advises "Don't be a cookie-cutter website." Although she uses an inexpensive template, she does the website herself.

Website Design

The design of your site should be simple yet comprehensive. By the time your customers have spent a few minutes on your website, they should have a pretty good sense of your business—not just what you sell but that you care about quality and customer service.

Your Homepage

Your customer will first come to your "homepage" where you will introduce them to your business and tempt them to spend some time on your site browsing other pages—and ultimately be enticed enough to order something.

Your homepage should introduce your business—go ahead and give a little history about how you got started but don't tell every detail about every thought you've ever had about the business. This is a chance for customers to feel like they know you but don't lose them right at the homepage!

Include a photo or two of your baskets on the homepage—the web customer should open to your site and know they got the site they are looking for. Go ahead and include a shot of you and your dog who accompanies you to work every day, but don't forget to show your baskets!

You don't need and don't want to show every basket you sell right on the front. The web page might take too long to load onto your potential customer's computer and they might move on to another website before they even see your baskets. Keep the homepage simple but informative.

By all means, do some advertising on this page. "Did you know that May 6th is National Nurses Day?" or some blurb that might make the viewer really think about ordering a basket can be great to push a viewing of your site to an actual order.

Include a menu of items along one edge of your homepage with headings that the customer can click on to get to that section of your online store. Think of it like the signs you see overhead in the grocery store or the pharmacy—direct customers to the sections they are interested in.

Drilling Down

Each time the viewer clicks on a button on your website they get further into your site. This can be accomplished in two ways—one is with a "pop-up window" where, when they click on a category, the new section pops up over the main page and when they are done browsing it and close it out, they get brought back to the page they started from. The other "drills" them further and further into your site. Drilling down like this is the most common way websites are set up but it can get frustrating to your customer if they can't easily get back to a point where they saw something they wanted to look at further. One way to help this is to always have a "home" button on every page—all they have to do is click "home" to get them back to the beginning and find their way forward again from there. It's like having Dorothy's ruby red slippers on your site at all times.

The Rest of the Site

Your homepage is one of the most important parts of your website. From there, you might want to show different kinds of baskets under different buttons on the home-page. So when a customer clicks on the "Holiday Baskets" button, they see samples of your baskets designed for Mother's Day, Christmas, Hanukkah, Easter, or whatever holidays you do baskets for. Other buttons might include "Men's Baskets," "Corporate Gifts," "Food Baskets," "Spa Baskets," or whatever categories of baskets you sell.

Some added-value pages you could add are things like a calendar showing all the national "celebration days" like Nurses Day and Doctors' Day and Grandparents Day. A page of "testimonials" from people who have received and enjoyed your baskets is always a good marketing tool. And you might have a few buttons that lead people to baskets by price—"$25," "$50–$100," etc.

You need a page for ordering, of course, which is covered in more detail below.

Like clothing e-stores where, with the click of the mouse, you can see your chosen sweater shown in a different color, perhaps customers can click on your Mother's Day basket to see the same basket transformed with different products.

> ## Beware!
> You can consider linking to the web pages of the companies whose products you include in your baskets, which would give customers information about the great products you are choosing to put in your high-quality baskets. But beware of leading customers away from your site—they may not come back. And beware of sending them to a site, say a soapmaker, who sells baskets of their own products. They may stop there and buy instead!

Selling from a Website

There was a time when small businesses used websites mainly as marketing pieces—people came to the site to view your products, then either called an order in or printed out a order form from the site and faxed their order to you. Those days are almost gone. Again, customers expect to be able to sit at their computer and not only see what you have to offer but be able to order it right then and there. If they can't, there is a good chance you are going to lose them to another basket site where they can.

The two key things that your site will need—and that your designer will set you up with—is a shopping cart for customers to collect their items in and a secure way to pay for them.

> ## Smart Tip
>
> Always include your business's name, address, and phone number on every page of your website. Once customers have drilled a few pages down into your site, they don't want to have to backtrack all the way back to your homepage just to get your contact information.

Shopping Cart

The shopping cart is a simple function that your web designer will build into your site if you say you want it (which you do). As your online customers shop, they can click the little button that says "add this item to my shopping cart" and it will join the list of any other items they have already put in the cart. Some carts accumulate items that stay there even after the customer has left the site. This feature can translate into more sales—if a customer gets interrupted before completing the transaction, they don't have to go through the entire shopping process when they return to your site. "Abandoned" shopping carts is a big issue with online shopping—customers leave before the sale is done—and this feature can retrieve some of those abandoned carts.

The shopping cart page is where the customer can make changes. Here they can change the quantity of each item (sometimes bad for you, when they decide to change it to 0, other times good when they decide not only will they order one of these baskets for their sister, but make it 3 and they'll send one to Mom and Aunt Jean as well).

Also on the shopping cart page will be where they decide what kind of shipping they want. Always offer inexpensive shipping options along with overnight options—shipping charges is one of those things that still bogs down catalog and online sales so give customers the option of making it very cheap. But you also want them to feel like they can shop online last minute as well, so the ability to have something shipped overnight is a must.

Payment Options

Most anyone reading this has shopped online and knows that credit cards are always an option for paying for your cyberpurchase. While using credit cards online has become very secure, there are still people who have no interest in giving out their credit card number over the internet. Some companies still give those people the option of faxing in their order or there is always the option of calling—both good reasons to make sure your contact information is available on all web pages.

PayPal is another option for paying online. People with a PayPal account load it up with funds and then funds are withdrawn when they use it to pay for a purchase online. PayPal payments are essentially electronic withdrawals from a checking account, allowing you to send money to anyone with an e-mail address. PayPal became the payment method of choice for eBay traders, so much so that in 2002 eBay bought PayPal. If you allow PayPal for purchase, your site will include a PayPal button.

Other Ways to Sell Online

There are other ways to sell your baskets online besides having your own website. You can try these in conjunction with your own site or before you get your site up and running.

Stat Fact

Gift Basket Review magazine's latest survey revealed the following top five challenges for the gift basket industry:

1. Competition from large merchants/discounters
2. Generating unique, fresh ideas for customers/clients
3. Rising gas and shipping costs
4. Rising cost of products
5. Getting good markups

These challenges remain whether you are a retail storefront or strictly a web business.

eBay

The popular auction site eBay offers a couple ways to sell your products online. You can list individual baskets in a "fixed price" listing where there is no actual bidding. Or you can sell them with "reserved pricing" where the item does not sell if it doesn't meet a minimum bid. Reserved pricing might be good on baskets that include one-of-a-kind items, like an autographed baseball or signed book.

The other way you can sell on eBay is to open an eBay store. This is basically a personalized selling platform similar to your own website, where eBay customers can come find your products. You must be an eBay seller already (which is a very easy process, with simple registration) and there is a nominal fee for the store. However, your products are potentially in front of the eyes of the millions of visitors to this very successful online selling space.

Other Sites

You might be able to work a deal with a website that sells complementary products that might carry your basket. Say your niche is the horse market and you are putting together an alternative-type basket using what is known as a "grooming tote"—a plastic, two-compartment container with a handle—and filling it with brushes, grooming products, a hoof pick, etc. See if one or more of the thousands of equine-related websites might carry your tote "basket" on their website for a share of the profit.

Dana Sonia, of Gift Baskets by Your Design in New Hampshire, has her own website but she is a very active business member of the state "NH Made" promotion. The state promotes products made in New Hampshire through a website that showcases members, provides links to their sites, and tells where the NH Made products can be found at retail sites run by the state (e.g., the larger state liquor stores have separate gift shops full of NH Made products).

Trades

If you already have your own website, you can consider finding appropriate sites with whom you can trade ads or products. For instance, "banner ads" (those mini-business-card-sized color ads you find around the edges of a website) are often traded among companies whose products and services complement each other. You can put hyperlinks on your website to other companies that you recommend and ask that they put your link on their site.

Marketing Your Website

Once you have created your website, don't keep it a secret! Be sure you web address is on every printed piece you create for your business—letterhead, business cards, gift enclosures, print advertisements, newsletters, radio

> **Tip...**
>
> **Smart Tip**
> Dana Sonia of Gift Baskets by Your Design in Chichester, New Hampshire, says that most of her customers find her via her website. "Almost 100 percent of my new business comes from my website," she says.

ads, everything that has to do with your business should announce your web address. Put the address in your answering machine message. Make sure it is on the door of your retail store so anyone walking by who either doesn't have time to come in or wanders by during your off hours knows they can find you on the internet.

▲

Get People Clicking

There's no point to having a website if you don't do what you can to get people to click on it. Here are some tips for attracting visitors, and possibly buyers, to your website:

- ◯ Simply tell all your friends and family and ask them to tell all their friends and family
- ◯ Do the appropriate search engine registration
- ◯ Make sure every printed and online piece you send to anyone has your website URL listed prominently
- ◯ Suggest visitors bookmark your site
- ◯ Trade web advertising with other websites
- ◯ Create contests with giveaways
- ◯ Change your content/product regularly to keep people coming back to see what's new
- ◯ Join online discussion groups
- ◯ If you do public speaking, always mention your site
- ◯ Provide an "expert" column to newspapers and make sure to mention your website

These are just a few of a long list of ideas for getting people to come to your website in the first place, keep coming back, and to encourage them to tell everyone they know. Click around to websites in the gift basket industry or in any category that interests you, see what catches your eye, and get other creative ideas to drive people to your site.

E-Newsletters

Creating a newsletter that is sent via e-mail has become a popular way for businesses to keep in touch with their customers. An e-mail newsletter is like a little reminder to your customers that you are there and waiting to fulfill their gift basket needs.

Solicit e-newsletter subscribers on your own website, and on the websites of others. Sending e-newsletters out unsolicited is considered "spam" and can land you in a bit of hot water. But once you create a useful, readable newsletter that might even contain a coupon or special or even a giveaway, people will readily subscribe.

Keep 'Em Interested

Once you get visitors checking out your site, there are some ways to keep them there as long as possible. The longer they are there, the more likely they are to order something.

Be sure they know immediately whose website they have gotten to. Make it easy for them to contact you by having a "contact us" button that makes it simple for them to send you a message.

Keep your website fun and changing. Do contests, include puzzles, whatever you can for fun interaction but always connect it to your gift basket business.

Provide site visitors with added value such as information sheets that have some connection with your baskets. For instance, if you are offering the "Healthy Breakfast Basket," include a fact sheet on your site that tells what is important about a healthy breakfast. (Don't forget to get permission and credit any information you use from elsewhere.)

Make it easy for customers to your website to order and pay. Nothing will make them click the exit button faster than to find it is difficult to spend their money!

Netiquette

The dramatic increase in the use of e-mail has meant that there is a need to understand good etiquette when it comes to e-mailing. The last thing you want to do is offend a customer. So follow these guidelines for proper e-mailing:

○ Never use all uppercase letters; it is considered the equivalent of shouting.

○ Spell-check your e-mails. Just because e-mail is quick, it doesn't have to be sloppy.

○ Give an accurate sense of what your e-mail is about in the subject line.

○ Create a signature for your e-mail so that every e-mail you compose automatically includes your business name, address, phone number, and e-mail address so the recipient can quickly see how to contact you.

○ Keep your messages short and to the point.

Don't Avoid Cyberspace

You can see that it is to your business's advantage to sell online. Once you become comfortable with computers and the internet and all the trappings that go with it, you will be surprised at how creatively you can use this marketing and selling option.

Sharon M. says one interesting market segment she's identified that uses her website are American expatriates—Americans living in foreign countries who want to send gifts to someone in the United States. Rather than making several overseas telephone calls, they'll surf the internet for a resource, looking for a company they feel comfortable with that carries products they like.

Because processing an order placed on her website is less expensive than through other methods, Sharon offers a 10 percent discount to customers who make their purchases online. Many regular customers who used to order by phone are switching to the web to save money and receive more efficient service. She is also seeing a steady increase in new customers who are discovering her on the internet. Another basketeer said her sales increased "five to six times" after she launched a website.

Fun Fact

A current trend in gift baskets is personalization and customization. Be sure your website makes it clear that you can mix and match products to make any of your standard baskets more custom to the recipient. But the more you customize, you need to price accordingly!

It does seem like a no-brainer to be selling online, but you must be prepared to deal with the additional sales. And although the costs for selling online can be very minor, they are still costs, such as website design and maintenance, that need to be figured into your overall projections and budget.

Financial
Management

One of the key indicators of the overall health of your business is its financial status, and it's important that you monitor your financial progress closely. The only way you can do that is to keep good records. There are a number of excellent computer accounting programs on the market, or you can handle the process manually. To create and maintain a set of books, you might want to ask your accountant for assistance in setting up your system. The key is to do that from the very beginning, and keep your records current and accurate throughout the life of your company. Keeping good records helps generate the financial statements that tell you exactly where you stand and what you need to do next.

Key Financial Statements

The key financial statements you need to understand and use regularly are:

- Profit and loss statement (also called the P&L or the income statement)
- Balance sheet
- Cash-flow statement

Profit and Loss Statement

This financial statement illustrates how much your company is making or losing over a designated period—monthly, quarterly, or annually—by subtracting expenses from revenue to arrive at a net result, which is either a profit or a loss.

This is where you can see how much income you are bringing in and compare it against how much in expenses you are paying out.

Except for cost of goods, which is specific to retailers and wholesalers (i.e., a gift basket business), the income statement for all businesses is essentially the same. They consist of income, gross profit margin, operating expenses, net profit (gross profit margin minus operating expenses), depreciation, net profit before interest (net profit minus depreciation), and interest (all interest accrued from short- and long-term debt).

Balance Sheet

A table showing your assets, liabilities, and capital at a specific point; a balance sheet is typically generated monthly, quarterly, or annually when the books are closed. Comparing balance sheets against past balance sheets in the same reporting period, you can pinpoint changes in your business's financial condition. This is the comparison that is being made when you hear on the news about a giant company whose earnings in a certain quarter were more or less than last year during that same quarter.

The top portion of the balance sheet lists assets, the bottom portion liabilities. Liabilities are reported as short-term (anything that needs to be paid within a year. such as sales commissions and taxes) and long-term (things that stretch out over a year, such a mortgage). Assets minus liabilities indicate your equity in your business.

Cash-Flow Statement

Summarizes the operating, investing, and financing activities of your business as they relate to the inflow and outflow of cash; as with the profit and loss statement, a cash-flow statement is prepared to reflect a specific accounting period, such as monthly, quarterly, or annually. A company showing a positive cash flow is not necessarily profitable, nor does a negative cash flow in any moment in time mean the business is not profitable. The latter in fact will most likely happen for any business that is seasonal in nature. This is a good reason to diversify your basket business so that you are not relying on just a few peak holidays but can have corporate orders taking up the slack the rest of the year.

See Appendix D for examples of these important statements. Successful basketeers review these reports regularly, at least monthly, so they always know where they stand and can quickly move to correct minor difficulties before they become major financial problems.

Record Keeping

It is important to retain your financial and other records for a period of time. Business tax records should be kept indefinitely as should financial statements. Employee documents, sales records, purchasing records, and travel records should be retained for four to six years.

Billing

If you're extending credit to your customers—and it's likely you will if you have corporate accounts—you need to establish and follow sound billing procedures.

Coordinate your billing system with your customers' payable procedures. Candidly ask what you can do to ensure prompt payment; that may include confirming the correct billing address and finding out what documentation may be required to help the customer determine the validity of the invoice. Keep in mind that many large companies pay certain types of invoices on certain days of the month; find out if your customers do that, and schedule your invoices to arrive in time for the next payment cycle.

If possible, bill on delivery. That's when the appreciation of your work is highest—whether the basket is being delivered to the customer who is paying the bill or somewhere else. When customers have just received an enthusiastic "thank you" from the recipient, they're thinking about you in a positive way, and they're more likely to process your invoice faster.

Beware!
Mail thieves operate even in the nicest of neighborhoods. If you receive checks in the mail, rent a post office box so you know they will be secure.

Most computer bookkeeping software programs include basic invoices. If you design your own invoices and statements, be sure they're clear and easy to understand. Detail each item and indicate the amount due in boldface type with the words "Please pay" in front of the total amount due. A confusing invoice may get set aside for clarification, and your payment will be delayed.

Finally, use your invoices as a marketing tool. Print reminders of upcoming holidays or gift-giving occasions on them. Add a flier or brochure to the envelope—even though the invoice is going to an existing customer, you never know where your brochures will end up.

Setting Credit Policies

When you extend credit to someone, you are essentially providing them with an interest-free loan. You wouldn't expect someone to lend you money without getting information from you about where you live and work as well as your potential ability

Taxing Matters

A critical administrative element in retail sales is the collection and remittance of sales tax. In addition to state sales tax, you may also need to collect a local sales tax. Your state department of revenue will provide you with complete instructions for dealing with sales tax.

Failing to collect and remit sales taxes can lead to serious consequences, including fines and even criminal charges. Some small-business owners think they are doing their customers a favor by not charging the appropriate sales tax, but in reality, you are breaking the law and taking a tremendous risk that could ultimately ruin your business.

If you operate by mail order, you may be required to collect and remit sales tax to the states where your customers reside. Check with your accountant for the latest rules on mail order sales tax requirements.

Remember: The sale isn't complete until the sales tax has been collected, reported, and paid to the proper government agency.

to repay. It just makes sense that you would want to get this information from someone you are lending money to.

Reputable companies will not object to providing you with credit information, or even paying a deposit on large orders. If you don't feel comfortable asking for at least part of the money upfront, just think how uncomfortable you'll feel if you deliver an expensive order and don't get paid at all. The business owners we talked to all agreed they felt awkward asking for deposits—until they got burned the first time; then it got much easier to ask.

> **Smart Tip** — *Tip...*
>
> Check the account status when taking an order from a customer on open credit. If the account is past due or the balance is unusually high, you may want to negotiate different terms before increasing the amount owed.

Certainly extending credit involves some risk, but the advantages of judiciously granted credit far outweigh the potential losses. Extending credit promotes customer loyalty. People will call you over a competitor because they already have an account set up and it's easy for them. Customers also often spend money more easily when they don't have to pay cash. Finally, if you ever decide to sell your business, it will have a greater value because you can show steady accounts.

Typically, you will only extend credit to commercial accounts. Individuals will likely pay cash (or by check) at the time of purchase, or use a credit card. You need to decide how much risk you are willing to take by setting limits on how much credit you will allow each account.

Your credit policy should include a clear collection strategy. Do not ignore overdue bills; the older a bill gets, the less likely it will ever be paid. Be prepared to take action on past-due accounts as soon as they're late.

Red Flags

Even though a customer passed your first credit check with flying colors doesn't mean you should never re-evaluate their credit status—in fact, you should do it on a regular basis.

Tell customers when you initially grant their credit application that you have a policy of periodically reviewing accounts, so when you do it, it's not a surprise. Remember, things can change very quickly in the business world, and a company that is on sound financial footing this year may be quite wobbly next year.

An annual re-evaluation of all customers on open account is a good idea—but if you start to see trouble in the interim, don't wait to take action. Another time to re-evaluate a customer's credit is when they request an increase in their credit line.

Some key trouble signs are a slowdown in payments, increased merchandise returns, and difficulty getting answers to your payment inquiries. Even a sharp increase in ordering could signal trouble; companies concerned that they may lose their credit privileges may try to stock up while they can. Pay attention to what your customers are doing; a major change in their customer base or product line is something you may want to monitor.

Take the same approach to a credit review that you would with a new credit application. Most of the time, you can use what you have on file to conduct the check, but if you are concerned for any reason, you may want to ask the customer for updated information.

Most customers will understand routine credit reviews and accept it as a sound business practice. A customer who objects may well have something to hide—and that's something you need to know.

Accepting Credit and Debit Cards

Whether your target market is corporate or individual consumers, you need to be able to accept credit and debit cards. Though many businesses prefer to be billed directly for corporate gift purchases, many more would rather charge the item to their personal or company credit card.

It's much easier now to get merchant status than it has been in the past. When Sue C. started her business 15 years ago, it took her almost a year to qualify for merchant status with the bank that had been handling her personal account for 20 years—and

Tax Time

Businesses are required to pay a wide range of taxes, and there are no exceptions for gift basket business owners. Keep good records so you can offset your local, state, and federal income taxes with the expenses of operating your company. If you have employees, you'll be responsible for payroll taxes. If you operate as a corporation, you'll have to pay payroll taxes for yourself; as a sole proprietor, you'll pay self-employment tax. Then there are property taxes, taxes on your equipment and inventory, fees and taxes to maintain your corporate status, your business license fee (which is really a tax), and other lesser-known taxes. Take the time to review all of your tax liabilities with your accountant.

every other bank she approached turned her down. Today, merchant status providers are competing aggressively for your business.

Sue C. keeps the credit card numbers of many of her customers—both corporate and individual—on file, and automatically charges their orders to their card.

Get approval on credit cards before you deliver the merchandise. This was a lesson Sue C. learned the hard way when a new customer called and ordered a $350 basket. "I had to go out and custom shop for it, and it took the entire day," she says. But when she finally processed the charge, she found out the credit card was stolen. Now she runs the credit card through first, and if the charge is denied, she calls the customer before delivering or shipping the basket.

To get a credit card merchant account, start with your own bank. Also check with various professional associations that offer merchant status as a member benefit. Shop around; this is a competitive industry, and it's worth taking the time to get the best deal.

Debit cards, which are designed to look like credit cards, are growing in popularity. Also called ATM cards, they actually withdraw the funds from the cardholder's account at the time the purchase is made. Getting debit card merchant status is typically somewhat easier than qualifying for credit card status; check with your local bank for the correct procedure.

> ### Smart Tip
> When tracking sales, break them down into basket types (holiday, sympathy, bridal, birthday, etc.) so you can quickly see where your strongest sales are.

Dealing with Your Own Creditors

Most business startup advice focuses on dealing with your customers, but you are also going to become a customer for your suppliers. That means you will have to pay for what you buy.

Find out in advance what your suppliers' credit policies are. Most will accept credit cards but will not put you on an open account until they've had a chance to run a check on you.

If you open an account with a supplier, be sure you understand their terms and preserve your credit standing by paying on time. Typically, you'll have 30 days to pay, but many companies offer a discount if you pay early.

> ### Dollar Stretcher
> Ask suppliers if payment terms can be a part of your price negotiation. For example, can you get a discount for paying cash in advance?

Income Statement

You should plan to keep track of the current financial status of your business using an income statement. Also referred to as a *profit and loss statement*, the income statement tracks the income and expenses of your business over a specific period of time, usually a month.

Don't forget to include prorated sums for anything you pay annually, such as subscriptions, licenses, or tax preparation. Put these into your expense lines as a monthly charge; so if you pay dues of $120/year to belong to a gift wire service, add $10 per month to your income statement as a line under the expense category.

Monthly Income Statement Worksheet

For the month of:		
Monthly Income		
Gross sales		
Cost of sales		
Gross Monthly Income		
Monthly Expenses		
Rent		
Phone/utilities		
Electronic card processing		
Employee payroll		
Postage		
Licenses		
Legal services		
Accounting services		
Office supplies		
Shipping supplies		
Insurance		
Subscriptions/dues		
Web hosting		
Internet service provider		
Loan repayment		
Miscellaneous		
Total Monthly Expenses		
Net Monthly Profit		

Sample Credit Application

Company Information

Company name _____

Address _____

_____

City _____ State _____ Zip _____

Phone _____ Fax _____ E-mail_____

Legal Status: Proprietorship ___ Partnership___ Corporation___ LLC___

Owners/Officers

1. Name _____ Title _____

   Address _____ Home phone _____

   City _____ State _____ Zip _____

1. Name _____ Title _____

   Address _____ Home phone _____

   City _____ State _____ Zip _____

Trade References

1. Company name _____

   Address _____

   _____

   City _____ State _____ Zip _____

   Phone _____ Fax _____

   Contact _____ Account # _____

2. Company name _____

   Address _____

   _____

   City _____ State _____ Zip _____

   Phone _____ Fax _____

   Contact _____ Account # _____

Bank Reference

1. Bank name _____

   Address _____

   _____

   City _____

   State _____ Zip _____

   Phone _____ Fax _____

   Contact _____ Account # _____

Sample Credit Application, continued

Credit Terms

Buyer agrees to the following:

○ To pay all invoices within terms shown on invoice (net 15 days).

○ To pay interest at 2.0 percent per month on all past-due accounts.

○ To pay cost of collection fees, including reasonable attorney fees.

○ Buyer further agrees that if Buyer is a corporation, the officer executing this agreement personally guarantees to pay the account of the Buyer.

○ On NSF checks, a $20 fee will be added to invoice/credit card payment.

Credit Policy

You must use a credit card to guarantee payment. Complete this section in addition to credit application for immediate shipment of your order. Your credit card will not be charged if payment of our invoice is received within 30 days.

Credit card # _____   Expiration date _____

Exact name on card _____

I have read, understood, and accept the above terms and have provided true information to the best of my knowledge.

Signed _____   Date _____

Print Name _____   Title _____

Tales
from the
Trenches

By now you should know how to get started and have a good idea of what to do—and what not to do—in your own gift basket business. But nothing teaches as well as the voice of experience. So we asked established gift basket business owners to tell us what has contributed to their success and what they think causes companies that don't make it to fail. Here are their stories.

Take Yourself and Your Business Seriously

Gift baskets can be a lot of fun to make, send, and receive—and many people don't realize what it really takes to make a business of them. "I think a lot of people who go into a gift basket business think it's easy and cute and creative, and all of their friends are going to use them, and they don't take it as seriously as another business," says Christine M. That, she says, is a sure prescription for failure.

You need a business plan, a marketing strategy, and a professional attitude. Christine is homebased and has children—and her children are not allowed in her office when she's working. First, there's the safety factor—many of the tools used to assemble baskets are dangerous weapons in a child's hands. Second, is the image issue. "I don't want my kids screaming in the background when I am on the phone," Christine says. "Another mother might laugh at it with me, but it makes corporate accounts nervous. It hurts the image of a homebased businessperson." Even though she's at home, she hires a sitter to watch the kids when she's working.

Give Yourself a Boost When You Need It

There is no way to avoid the occasional bad day—the day when deliveries don't arrive, customers are complaining, and you're making mistakes. Stop and give yourself a pat on the back.

Sue C. does this by pulling out what she calls her "love letters" file. It's where she keeps all the complimentary cards and notes she has received from customers over the years. "You don't often get personal thank-you notes, so it's a big deal to me when I get one, and I keep them," she says. "Whenever I feel like I've done something wrong, or I'm not going in the right direction, or if I have a bad day, I'll go through that love-letter file. Those notes tell me I have touched those people in a positive way. And I remind myself that I can't please everybody all of the time no matter how hard I try."

Keep Learning

Take advantage of all the information and training opportunities you can. Your local Small Business Development Center can not only help you with startup information but also provide classes and counseling to help you manage and grow your business once it's established. Most business-oriented chambers of commerce offer seminars that focus on hot

> **Tip...**
>
> **Smart Tip**
>
> Steal ideas shamelessly. Look at what other successful gift basketeers are doing and apply their techniques to your business. Also study all kinds of successful companies and think about how you can adapt their methods to your operation.

business topics. Attend trade shows and conventions, and take advantage of the workshops they offer.

Subscribe to industry-specific and general business publications. You don't have to read every word of every issue; just skim the table of contents and read the articles that are appropriate to your situation. Also, read the business section of your local newspaper and your local business journal—this is especially important if you are targeting the corporate market. Also on your reading list should be business books that will give you ideas to run and grow your business.

> **Bright Idea**
> Learn from big corporations. You may not think you have much in common with corporate giants, but these companies started out as small, entrepreneurial operations. Find out what they did to become so successful.

Listen to people. Most people love to give advice; you may have to filter out a good deal of what you hear, but listen anyway.

Most important, learn from your mistakes. "I wish I had a dollar for all the little mistakes I've made," says Claire S. But rather than fretting about having made a mistake, she learns from the situation and moves on.

Be Accessible

It's been called the "microwave mentality"—when people want something, they want it now. Make it easy for customers to talk to you when they want to and even easier for them to place orders whether you're available or not.

If you are a solo operator, a cellular phone is a must. It not only makes you accessible, it gives you a tool to maximize the time you spend in the car. "I am always able to be reached on my cell phone," says Sue C. "I've had many customers tell me that the main reason they call me is they know they can always talk to me personally."

Set up a 24-hour dedicated fax line, and let customers know they can fax orders to you any time, at their convenience.

Take Their Breath Away

Create stunningly beautiful baskets. You want people to gasp and be truly delighted when presented with one of your baskets.

Sue C. puts it this way: "I'm not in business to make money. My job, my spiritual job, is to touch as many people as I possibly can. This business is my vehicle, and from that business, money comes."

Success in the gift basket business comes from being truly committed and having a passion for making people happy every single day. Says Claire S., "Your heart and soul have to go into it."

Market Your Business Constantly

Be sure everybody you know and everybody you meet knows what you do. Always have business cards with you, and don't be shy about handing them out.

You also need a backup plan. If your original marketing strategy isn't producing the results you want, think about how you can adjust it for a better outcome.

Smart Tip

Tip...

Do an annual review of your company. At the end of each year, give your company a complete and thorough checkup to make sure you're on track. Review your financial reports, inventory records, insurance coverage, employment policies, and general operations.

Don't Market by Price

People want value for their dollar. You have to respect your customers' budgets, but marketing based on price is the kiss of death to a gift basket business. You need to charge enough money to make a reasonable profit; otherwise, you won't stay in business.

Stay Focused and Organized

Especially when you're homebased, it's easy to let your personal life cross over to your business, and vice versa. Exercise the necessary discipline to remain focused on your business and keep your operation organized.

When you are first starting out, Dana S. of Gift Baskets by Your Design in New Hampshire recommends not getting "overexcited and going out and buying lots of stuff. Think of specifics, think of a few designs at first and build on that. We started out specializing in New Hampshire." New Hampshire products are still the focus of a line of Dana's baskets, but she will create baskets with a wide range of products from soaps to chocolates.

Enhance Your Gift Basket Service with Extras

In addition to creating original custom gift baskets, Christine M. offers a personal shopping service to her customers. If they want something special and she doesn't have it, she'll find it.

Guarantee Your Work

If someone isn't satisfied with a basket, for whatever reason, make it right.

Get Feedback

Ask your clients for feedback about your work—the level of service you provide as well as the quality of the baskets—and accept criticism gracefully.

When a client takes the trouble to let you know how you can improve, be sure to express your appreciation and let them know what you've done to correct the problem.

Establish and Maintain Flawless Credit

A good credit rating is one of the most valuable assets a business can have. Suppliers appreciate customers who pay on time, and they'll always be willing to help you with a special need. Claire S. says her suppliers will overnight urgent orders and only charge her for ground freight because her track record with them is so strong. "If your credit is good, your vendors will work with you," she says. "But if you play games and you lose their trust, when you really need something in a pinch, you won't get it."

Trade and Barter Whenever Possible

You have a product a lot of people want, so use your product instead of cash whenever possible. Whenever you're buying products or services from another small business, ask if they're interested in negotiating a trade. Your mechanic may accept a gift basket in exchange for changing your oil. Your dentist may take one as payment for cleaning your teeth. It doesn't hurt to ask; the worst that can happen is that they'll say no, and you'll pay cash. Just remember that bartering arrangements must be reported to the IRS, so check with your accountant to make sure you are in compliance with the law.

Play by the Rules

Like it or not, businesses in the United States are heavily regulated. When you're in business, you have a legal and ethical obligation to comply with those regulations. It may not seem like a big deal to buy a bottle of champagne and put it in someone's gift basket, but if you don't have a liquor license,

> **Bright Idea**
> When what you thought was a good idea flops, take the time to figure out why. Then, if appropriate, adjust your strategy and try again.

it's against the law. You might think it's absurd that the health department will want to inspect your kitchen when you're baking homemade cookies to include in your food baskets, but if someone gets sick from your food, failure to comply with those requirements will only add to your liability. And you may think you're doing someone a favor by not charging and collecting sales tax, but the state sees that as stealing.

Beyond the liability and the consequences of failing to follow regulations, Claire S. says it's also a question of fairness. Legitimate gift basket businesses pay multiple layers of taxes, pass numerous health- and safety-related inspections, and refuse to skirt the law, even though it could mean additional profits. When basketeers—either deliberately or through ignorance—fail to operate by the same standards, it damages the industry as a whole.

Appendix A
Gift Basket
Resources

They say you can never be rich enough or thin enough. While these could be argued, you really can never have enough resources. Therefore, here are some helpful sources for you to check into, check out, and harness for your own personal information blitz.

These sources are tidbits, ideas to get you started on your research. They are by no means the only sources out there and they should not be taken as the Ultimate Answer. These have been updated for this new edition, but things change faster than books get into print, so don't be surprised if some things have changed. Get out and start investigating.

If you haven't yet joined the Internet Age, stop pretending it's not for you and just do it! The internet provides a breathtaking array of resources literally at your fingertips.

Associations

Gift Association of America, 115 Rolling Hills Rd., Johnstown, PA 15905-5225, (814) 288-1460, fax: (814) 288-1483, giftassn.com

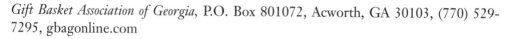
Gift Basket Association of Georgia, P.O. Box 801072, Acworth, GA 30103, (770) 529-7295, gbagonline.com

Gift Basket Exchange Network, gbexchange.net

National Specialty Gift Association, 7238 Bucks Ford Dr., Riverview, FL 33569, (813) 671-4757, fax: (813) 677-5075, nsgaonline.com

Consultants and Other Experts

Robert S. Bernstein, Esq., Bernstein Law Firm P.C., 1133 Penn Ave., Pittsburgh, PA 15222, (412) 456-8101, fax: (412) 456-8135, e-mail: bob@bernsteinlaw.com

Allen Konopacki, Ph.D., trade-show consultant, Incomm Research Center, 5574 North Northwest Highway, Chicago, IL 60630, (312) 642-9377, tradeshowresearch.com

Equipment Suppliers

All Cart Manufacturing Inc., custom designed and manufactured carts, kiosks, and other custom vending vehicles, 1450 Universal Rd., Columbus, OH 43207, (800) 695-2278, (614) 443-5544, fax: (614) 443-4248, e-mail: jjmorris@allacart.com, www.allacart.com

Cart and Kiosk.com, custom design and manufacture of retail merchandising fixtures, kiosks, carts, and interactive displays, 218 Ranchitos, Corrales, NM 87048, (505) 897-1206, fax: (505) 898-7005, cartandkiosk.com

Jetram Sales Inc., wrapping and packaging supplies and equipment, 4429 Ridgewood, St. Louis, MO 63116, (800) 551-2626, (314) 351-5533, fax: (314) 781-0192, e-mail: jetram1@aol.com, jetramsales.com

ProPack Inc., shrink-film packaging equipment and supplies, 196 Coolidge Ave., Englewood, NJ 07631, (201) 871-8787, fax (201) 871-8908, shrinkfilm.com

ATW Manufacturing Co. Inc., PacWrap shrink-wrapping system, 4065 W. 11th Ave., Eugene, OR 97401, (800) 759-3388, atwmfg.com

Franchise and Business Opportunities

Baskets Plus, 207 A Livingston St., Northvale, NJ 07647, (201) 768-8860, fax: (201) 768-7077, baskets-plus.com

Candy Bouquet, Candy Bouquet International Inc., 423 East Third St., Little Rock, AR 72201, (877) 266-3901, (501) 375-9990, fax: (501) 375-9998, candybouquet.com

Internet Resources

America Online's Business Know-How Forum has a Gift Basket and Balloon Forum with a message board, library, and weekly chats. Visit AOL for information on days and times.

Gift Basket Supply Vendors Directory, giftbasketsupplyvendors.com, offers a list of hundreds of vendors, website design and hosting, marketing tips, trade-show information, a holiday calendar, and more.

Inventory Suppliers

Baskets Unlimited, 4826 S. Santa Fe, Vernon, CA 90058, (323) 581-0111, fax: (323) 581-3584, e-mail: bultd@yahoo.com

BoxCo, creative boxes that can serve as an alternative to baskets, 10875 NW 52nd St., #2, Sunrise, FL 33351, (800) 654-2932, boxcoindustries.com

Clippermill, wire breadbaskets, mini shopping carts, mini colanders, 404 Talbert St., San Francisco, CA 94014, (415) 330-2400, fax: 415-330-9640, e-mail: info@clipper mill.com, clippermill.com

Creative Cookie Etc., specialty fortune cookies, 8673 Commerce Drive, Suite 7, Easton, MD 21601, (800) 451-4005, (410) 819-0091, fax: (410) 819-0255, creative cookie.com

David Alan Chocolatier, Swiss-style truffles, 1700 N. Lebanon St., Lebanon, IN 46052-0588, (800) 428-2310, fax: (765) 482-5660, davidalanchocolatier.com

Flowers Inc., balloons, gift accessories, and baskets, 325 Cleveland Rd., Bogart, GA 30622, (800) 241-2094, (706) 548-1588, fax: (800) 880-9759, burtonandburton.com

Imperial Foods Inc., gourmet foods for gift baskets, 2855 Shermer Rd., Northbrook, IL 60062, (800) 729-8116, e-mail: info@imperial-foods.com, imperial-foods.com

Metrovox Snacks, LLC, parent company of Fontazzi, Snack Works and Barravox, 6116 Walker Ave., Maywood, CA 90270, (888) 224-7110, fax: (888) 865-3639, giftbasket supplies.com

Neighbors Coffee, specialty coffees, gourmet hot chocolate, instant cappuccino mixes, and gourmet teas, 11 N.E. 11th St., Oklahoma City, OK 73104, (800) 299-9016, (405) 236-3932, neighborscoffee.com

Specialty Wraps Etc., packaging supplies, shred, bows, ribbons, tissue sheets, bags, shrink products, and more, 2230 Oneida St., Clayville, NY 13322-0162, (315) 839-5557, fax: (315) 839-5457, specialtywraps.com

▲

Stephan Enterprises, baby gifts and accessories, 3 Pequignot Dr., Pierceton, IN 46562, (800) 359-2917, fax (514) 594-2215, stephanbaby.net

Magazines and Publications

Gift Basket Review, 815 Haines St., Jacksonville, FL 32206, (800)729-6338, www.festivities-pub.com

Gifts and Decorative Accessories, (336) 605-1034, giftsandec.com

Giftware News, Talcott Communications, 20 W. Kinzie, Suite 1200, Chicago, IL 60610, (312) 849-2220, fax: (312) 849-2174, giftwarenews.net

Rave Reviews Magazine, basketconnection.com

Specialty Retail Report, 195 Hanover St., Hanover, MA 02339, (800) 936-6297, www.specialtyretail.com

Business Resources

America's Small Business Development Center Network, asbdc-us.org

American Association of Franchisees and Dealers, P.O. Box 81887, San Diego, CA 92138-1887, (800) 733-9858, e-mail: Benefits@AAFD.org, aafd.org

Federal Trade Commission, CRC-240, Washington, DC 20580, (877) FTC-HELP, ftc.gov

National Association for the Self-Employed (nase.org), P.O. Box 612067, DFW Airport, Dallas, TX 75261-2067, (800) 232-6273

National Association of Women Business Owners, 830-1100 Wayne Avenue, Silver Spring, MD 20910, (301) 608-2590, nawbo.org

Service Corps of Retired Executives (SCORE), National Office, 409 Third St., SW, 6th Floor, Washington DC 20024, (800) 634-0245, score.org

U.S. Chamber of Commerce, 1615 H Street NW, Washington, DC 20062-2000, (202) 659-6000, uschamber.com

U.S. Small Business Administration (sba.gov), 409 Third Street, SW, Washington, DC 20416, answer desk (800) 827-5722, e-mail: answerdesk@sba.gov

Appendix B
Naming Worksheet

Perhaps you'd like to name your business something completely unique but don't know where to start. Here is a worksheet to help you with some things you should consider:

What are the first three things that pop into your head when you think of a gift? Things like "holiday," "special," or "love" would be examples.

1. _____

2. _____

3. _____

What are the first three things you think of when you think of the idea of a basket?

1. _____

2. _____

3. _____

Are there landmarks in your area or natural features about your location or anything unique that characterizes where you are? The Golden Gate Bridge, "seaside," or "country lane" might be examples.

1. _____

2. _____

3. _____

Play around with these different elements; mix and match them to see if a name pops out as a good one. You want to avoid using a location as your business name if you think you may move someday, since Green Bay Gift Baskets may seem odd in Milwaukee. You certainly should consider using your own name for a business name (Susie's Gift Baskets).

Whatever you come up with, say it out loud a few times. Tell your friends to call so you can answer the phone with your potential name and see how, or if, it rolls off your tongue. And ask your friends how it sounded on the other end. Is it a mouthful? Could they understand what you were saying?

Once you've landed on something you think works, don't get stationery or checks printed up until you check with the state or county registry to make sure it isn't taken. Even if you have searched it in the local phone book or online, someone could have registered it but not started using it yet.

Appendix C
Checklists

This appendix contains several checklists that will be helpful with things like determining trends in the gift basket business, planning your marketing campaigns, and deciding on a retail location.

Tracking Trends

Emerging trends can have an impact on your business—both good and bad. Stay informed to keep abreast of the changing gift market, both to keep your business ideas fresh and to avoid a disaster like investing in a supply of purple widgets from a business that is closing only to find that purple was in but now is way out. Here are some ideas to keep yourself in the know:

❏ *Read a local newspaper or two to keep up with local trends and changes, but also read national news.* Your reading choice will depend on your market—*USA Today* will give you the pulse of the middle-class while *The Financial Times* will tell you what the more well-to-do investor types are thinking these days. Look at ads for style trends and to get a sense of what people are interested in.

❑ *Join associations that serve the gift basket and small-business industry.* Gift-related associations are an excellent source of current news geared specifically to businesses like yours. Check the "associations" section of appendix A in this book.

❑ *Keep an eye on what kinds of nonfiction books are selling well.* What is the general population reading? Pets are currently hot—is it time to offer a pampered pet gift basket?

❑ *Contact government agencies or consult government publications for specific questions.* The Departments of Commerce and Labor and the Census Bureau, for instance, may have data indicating various trends. You might also consult large libraries with sections devoted to government publications, but these days you can do a lot of this research online.

❑ *Contact manufacturers, wholesalers, and distributors that service the gift industry.* They can furnish information not only on the products they provide but also on trends in the industry that they've discovered from their own market research. Talk to their salespeople who call on you and find out what trends they are seeing out in the field.

❑ *Check your library to see if they subscribe to an online information service.* They are often too expensive for a small business to subscribe to, but larger libraries often carry subscriptions for their patrons' use.

❑ *Subscribe to gift-related and crafts-related magazines and newsletters.* Many trade associations publish trade periodicals that report on their particular industry. These publications are usually filled with valuable management tips, industry trends, buying guides, etc.

Market Planning Checklist

Before you launch a marketing campaign, answer the following questions about your business and your product or service.

- ❏ Have you analyzed the gift basket market? Do you know which features of your service will appeal to which market segments?

- ❏ In forming your marketing message, have you made sure to describe how your product will benefit your customers?

- ❏ Have you prepared a pricing schedule? Have you decided what kinds of discounts you will offer and to whom you will offer them?

- ❏ Have you prepared a sales forecast?

- ❏ Which media will you use in your marketing campaign?

- ❏ Have you planned any sales promotions?

- ❏ Have you planned a publicity campaign?

- ❏ Do your marketing materials mention any optional accessories or added services—a "gift basket subscription," for example—that consumers might want to purchase?

- ❏ What kind of customer service do you provide to back up your products?

- ❏ Do you have liability insurance in case a product causes an allergic reaction or a child basket ends up with something in it that is a choking hazard?

- ❏ Does your planned packaging appeal to your target market?

- ❏ How will you distribute your baskets?

- ❏ Have you prepared job descriptions for any employees needed to carry out your marketing campaign/plan?

Retail Location Checklist

If you plan to operate your gift basket business out of a retail location, the following checklist will help you in your search for the best location. Answer the questions by indicating whether the item is a strength (S) or a weakness (W) of the potential site as it specifically relates to your business. Once you have completed the checklist for each prospective location, compare the relative strengths and weaknesses to help determine which location best suits the potential success of your business.

	S	W
Is the site large enough for your business needs?	❏	❏
Does it meet your layout requirements?	❏	❏
Does the building need any repairs?	❏	❏
Will you have to make any leasehold improvements?	❏	❏
Will you have to do any electrical, plumbing, or ventilation work?	❏	❏
Is the site easily accessible to your prospective customers?	❏	❏
Can you find qualified employees in the area?	❏	❏
Is the facility consistent with the image you wish to project?	❏	❏
Is the site in a safe neighborhood with a low crime rate?	❏	❏
Are there neighboring businesses that might attract customers who will also patronize your business?	❏	❏
Are there any competitors nearby? If so, can you successfully compete with them?	❏	❏
Can suppliers conveniently make deliveries to this location?	❏	❏
If your business expands in the future, will the facility be able to accommodate this growth?	❏	❏
Are the lease terms and rent favorable?	❏	❏
Is the location zoned for a retail business?	❏	❏

Checklist of Existing Resources

Chances are you may already own or have access to some of the things you will need in your business. Perhaps a friend has a business that has certain equipment you could borrow, at least until you can budget in to purchase your own. It's not a bad idea to plan to eventually become fully equipped, if for no other reason than to be prepared to sell the business. But it also doesn't hurt to budget purchase of some equipment for after you've started to bring in some revenue.

Here's a list of somthings to consider:

❏ *Computer equipment: Do you have a computer that you can readily use for the business?* This is especially likely if you plan to have your gift basket business homebased. Or maybe you have a laptop computer that would suffice and in the meantime you can spend your money on a higher-quality printer that is dedicated to the business.

❏ *Where do you plan to warehouse your basket supplies?* This includes baskets, which can be a bulky storage item, as well as other common products you might use in your regular offerings such as soaps, tea, tins of crackers, lotions, cloth handkerchiefs, or whatever. Do you have space somewhere in your home that you could carve out? Do you have a neighbor who used to store items for his business that he sold and now the shed is empty? Don't be afraid to be creative, but also make sure the storage is convenient for you. Whatever you decide for bulk storage, you will need enough room in your work space—whether it is at home or a retail location—for your day-to-day supplies.

❏ *Are you one of those people who are always involved in activities and organizations?* These are existing resources in the form of useful contacts for drumming up business or locating something you need. Don't be afraid to use them; they are often happy to help.

❏ *Office/shop furniture: The gift basket business is typically a homey, craftsy-type business.* Customers will not expect your shop to look like a hi-tech store. You can use dressers and bookcases and wood tables to display your wares. Look around your home, your friends' and family's attics. Think creatively! You don't need to buy expensive furnishings—in fact, save your budget to buy just what you need to make a superefficient work area.

▲

Business Evaluation Checklist

You may be looking at buying an existing gift basket business. Here are some things to consider before signing on the dotted line:

❑ Why does the current owner want to sell the business?

❑ Does the business have potential for future growth?

❑ If the business has been in decline, will you be able to salvage it and make it successful?

❑ Is the business in sound financial condition? Have you seen audited year-end financial statements for the business? Have you reviewed the most recent statements? Have you reviewed the business's tax returns for the past five years?

❑ Have you seen copies of all the business's current contracts?

❑ Is the business currently involved in a lawsuit? Has it ever been involved in a lawsuit? If so, what is the status or what was the result?

❑ Does the business have any debts or liens against it? If so, what are they for and in what amounts?

❑ What percentage of the business's accounts are past due? How much does the business write off each year for bad debts?

❑ How many customers does the business serve on a regular basis?

❑ Who makes up the market for the business? Where are the customers located?

❑ Does any single customer account for a large portion of the sales volume? If so, would the business be able to survive without this customer? Is it likely you will retain this customer when you buy the business?

❑ How does the business market its baskets?

❑ Does the business have exclusive rights to market any particular products or services? If so, how has it obtained this exclusivity? Is it making the best possible use of this exclusivity? Do you have written proof that the current business owner can transfer this exclusivity to you?

❑ Are the business' supplies, merchandise, and other materials available from several suppliers, or are there only a handful who can meet the business's needs? If you lost the business's current supplier, what impact would that loss have on the business? Would you be able to find substitute goods of appropriate quality and price?

- ❑ Are there any aspects about this basket business that are in danger of becoming obsolete or are "fads"? (i.e., if you bought a business that was exclusively into selling baskets that focused on movies on videotape, you would be in trouble!)

- ❑ What is the business's market share?

- ❑ What competition does the business face? How can the business compete successfully? Have the business's competitors changed recently? Have any of them gone out of business, for instance?

- ❑ Does the business have all the equipment you think is necessary? Will you need to add or update any equipment?

- ❑ What is the business's current inventory worth? Will you be able to use any of this inventory, or is it inconsistent with your intended product line?

- ❑ How many employees does the business have? What positions do they hold?

- ❑ Does the business pay its employees high wages, or are the wages average or low?

- ❑ Does the business experience high employee turnover? If so, why?

- ❑ What benefits does the business offer its employees?

- ❑ Will the change of ownership cause any changes in personnel?

You can see where this checklist could also be used if you were looking to get your business in shape to sell it. It is never too early to think about your business from this perspective; some of these things take years to establish.

Real Estate Lease Checklist

Once you have just about decided on a site, check the following before you sign the lease:

- ❑ Is there sufficient electrical power? Enough electrical outlets of the right kind (i.e., grounded, ground-fault for near water sources, 220-volt for some higher-powered equipment like clothes dryers)?
- ❑ Is there enough parking space for customers and employees?
- ❑ Is there sufficient lighting? Heating? Air conditioning?
- ❑ Do you know the specifics of the kind of sign you can erect? Whether there are size limitations, height limitations, whether it can be lighted, etc.
- ❑ Will the city's zoning allow your business in that site?
- ❑ Will the landlord approve the alterations you feel are necessary?
- ❑ Must you pay to return the site to its original condition when you move out?
- ❑ Is there any indication that the roof leaks?
- ❑ Is the cost of burglary insurance high in that area?
- ❑ Can you secure the building at a reasonable cost against the threat of burglary?
- ❑ Will the health department approve your business at this site?
- ❑ Will the fire department approve the operation of your business at this location?
- ❑ Have you included a written description of the real property?
- ❑ Have you attached drawings of the property to the lease document?
- ❑ Do you have written guidelines for renewal terms?
- ❑ Do you know when your lease payments begin?
- ❑ Have you bargained for one to three months' free rent?
- ❑ Do you know your date of possession?
- ❑ Have you listed the owner's responsibility for improvements?
- ❑ Do you pay the taxes?
- ❑ Do you pay the insurance?
- ❑ Do you pay the maintenance fee?
- ❑ Do you pay the utilities?
- ❑ Do you pay the sewer fees?
- ❑ Have you asked your landlord for a cap of 5 percent on your rent increases?
- ❑ Have you included penalty clauses in case the project is late and you are denied occupancy?
- ❑ Have you retained the right to obtain your own bids for signage?
- ❑ What are the terms for getting out of the lease?
- ❑ Has your attorney reviewed the contract?

Insurance Planning Worksheet

All of these insurances are not necessary for every business, but they all are worth asking about. Only you can decide how much risk you can afford to take on.

Types of Insurance	Required? (Y/N)	Yearly Cost	Cost per Payment
General liability insurance			
Product liability insurance			
Errors and omissions liability insurance			
Malpractice liability insurance			
Automotive liability insurance			
Fire and theft insurance			
Business interruption insurance			
Overhead expense insurance			
Personal disability			
Key-employee insurance			
Shareholders' or partners' insurance			
Credit extension insurance			
Term life insurance			
Health insurance			
Group insurance			
Workers' compensation insurance			
Survivor-income life insurance			
Care, custody, and control insurance			
Consequential losses insurance			
Profit insurance			
Money and securities insurance			
Glass insurance			
Electronic equipment insurance			
Power interruption insurance			
Rain insurance			
Temperature damage insurance			
Transportation insurance			
Fidelity bonds			
Surety bonds			
Title insurance			
Water damage insurance			
TOTAL ANNUAL COSTS		$	$

Pricing Checklist

Pricing a product is one of the most important business decisions you will make. Pricing gift baskets isn't quite as simple as pricing a single item that you purchase from a wholesaler and mark up the appropriate percentage to meet your profit requirements. Since baskets consist of not only multiple items but multiple components that comprise the construction of the basket, pricing is a bit more complex.

Use the following checklist to come up with your price on each of your baskets:

❑ Cost of basket/container: $_____

❑ Cost of the construction:
    Shred: $_____
    Shrink wrapping: $_____
    Bows/ribbon: $_____
    Gift tag: $_____
    Cellophane: $_____
    Other: $_____

❑ Cost of contents:
    1. _____ $_____
    2. _____ $_____
    3. _____ $_____
    4. _____ $_____
    5. _____ $_____
    6. _____ $_____
    7. _____ $_____
    8. _____ $_____
    9. _____ $_____
    10. _____ $_____

❑ **Total Cost of Contents:** $_____
(You may have more or fewer items than this, depending on the size of the basket, but don't forget to list every item that is a different cost, and if there are more than one, be sure to multiply the cost times the number of those items in the basket.)

❑ **Total Cost of Basket/Construction/Contents:** $_____

❑ Cost of your time: $_____
(total minutes/hours you spent creating the basket multiplied by the hourly rate you want to get)

❑ What are the average "incidentals" in creating a basket: $_____
(This is a figure for items like tape, staples, glue, etc. that you should calculate on the side and have at hand for different sizes/types of baskets.)

❑ Markup (as a percentage) _____%: $_____

Total Cost of This Basket: $_____

Business Plan Checklist

- ❑ Title Page
- ❑ Executive Summary
- ❑ Table of Contents
- ❑ Description of Your Business:
  - ❑ What product or service you will provide
  - ❑ Where you will be located
  - ❑ What is your competition?
  - ❑ What is the management arrangement and organization of your business?
- ❑ Market Analysis and Marketing Plan
  - ❑ Description of the gift basket market
  - ❑ Your target market
  - ❑ Analysis of the competition
  - ❑ Customer characteristics
  - ❑ Overall sales plan
- ❑ Financial Data, including:
  - ❑ Any capital equipment needs or assets already owned
  - ❑ Sources of funding
  - ❑ Balance sheet
  - ❑ Cash flow pro forma for one year
  - ❑ Pro forma income statement for three years
  - ❑ Past financial history
  - ❑ Personal financial information (esp. if you are a sole proprietorship)
- ❑ Supporting Documents
  - ❑ Resumes of any key personnel
  - ❑ Personal cost-of-living budget
  - ❑ Contracts and legal documents pertaining to the business
  - ❑ Any market research documentation—articles, statistics sources, etc.

Customer Information Questionnaire

1. Have you ever given a basket as a gift to anyone before?   Y   N

   If so, how many times per year do you give gift baskets as gifts? _____

2. On what occasions do you find giving a gift basket appropriate?

   ___ Christmas   ___ Valentine's Day   ___ Mother's Day

   ___ Birthday   ___ Thank-you gift   ___ Get well

3. To whom do you usually give gift baskets?

   ___ Female relative   ___ Female friend   ___ Female coworker/employee

   ___ Male relative   ___ Male friend   ___ Male coworker/employee

4. What kinds of things do you think are appropriate for gift baskets?

   ___ Homemade food   ___ Fresh produce   ___ Flowers

   ___ Books or magazines   ___ Canned goods (jams, etc.)

   ___ Small gift items   ___ Other ideas?

5. What do you think is a good price for a gift basket?

   ___ $15–20   ___ $30–50   ___ Over $100

   ___ $20–30   ___ $50–100

6. Rank your considerations when choosing a gift basket:

   ___ Contents   ___ Price   ___ Looks

7. If there was a gift basket shop in your area, would you give baskets as gifts? Y   N

8. What is your preferred way of ordering/buying a gift basket?

   ___ In person in a retail store   ___ On the phone

   ___ From a print catalog   ___ From a website

Thank you!

Appendix D
Financial Worksheets

Every business, no matter how big or small, sho~~~ ~
appropriate financial statements and fore~~~
ness's viability at any given t~~~
single basket! In this appe~~~
help you with the financial

Total Liabilities		
Net Worth (A – B = C)		
Total Liabilities & Net Wor~~~		

Personal Balance Sheet

Personal Balance Sheet as of _____ , 20_____

Assets		Totals
Cash, checking, & savings		
Marketable securities		
Real estate owned: home, vacation, or rental property		
Partial interest in real estate equities		
Automobiles		
Personal property (jewelry, artwork, and so on)		
Personal loans outstanding		
Cash value/life insurance		
Other assets/itemize		
Total Assets	A	

Liabilities		Totals
Secured loans (car, home improvements, equipment)		
Unsecured loans		
Charge account bills		
...l estate mortgages		
...d income tax		
...ts/itemize		
	B	
	C	
...h (B + C)	D	

Personal Financial Statement

Statement of Financial Condition as of _____, 20__

Individual Information	Coapplicant Information
Name	Name
Home address	Home address
City, state, & zip	City, state, & zip
Name of employer	Name of employer
Title/position	Title/position
Years with employer	Years with employer
Employer address	Employer address
City, state ,& zip	City, state, & zip
Home phone Business phone	Home phone Business phone

Source of Income	Totals	Contingent Liabilities	Totals
Salary (applicant)		If guarantor, comaker, or endorser	
Salary (coapplicant)		If you have any legal claims	
Bonuses & commissions (applicant)		If you have liability for a lease or contract	
Bonuses & commissions (coapplicant)		If you have outstanding letters of credit	
Income from rental property		If you have outstanding surety bonds	
Investment income		If you have any contested tax liens	
Other income*		If you listed an amount for any of the above, give details:	
Total Income			

*Income from alimony, child support, or separate maintenance income need not be revealed if you do not wish to have it considered as a basis for repaying this obligation.

Assets	Totals	Liabilities	Totals
Cash, checking, & savings		Secured loans	
Marketable securities		Unsecured loans	
Nonmarketable securities		Charge account bills	
Real estate owned/home		Personal debts	
Partial interest in real estate equities		Monthly bills	
Automobiles		Real estate mortgages	
Personal property		Unpaid income tax	
Personal loans		Other unpaid taxes and interest	
Cash value—life insurance		Other debts—itemize	
Other assets—itemize			
		Total Liabilities	
		Net Worth	
Total Assets		Total Liabilities & Net Worth	

▲

Personal Cash-Flow Statement

Statement of Financial Condition as of _____, 20__

Monthly Variable Expenses		Totals
Grocery purchases		
Automobiles: gasoline, repairs, servicing		
Utility bills: electricity, water, phone, etc.		
Clothing		
Medical, dental, prescriptions		
Entertainment		
Other monthly variable expenses—itemize		
Total Variable Expenses	A	

Monthly Fixed Expenses		Totals
Rent or mortgage payment		
Auto loan: car 1		
Auto loan: car 2		
Credit card payment 1		
Credit card payment 2		
Credit card payment 3		
Credit card payment 4		
Major store accounts		
Donations		
Insurance payments		
Home improvement loans—itemize		
Total Fixed Expenses	B	
Total Monthly Expenses (A + B = C)	C	

Monthly Income			
	Gross income	D	
	Payroll deductions	E	
	Net income (D – E)	F	
	Disposable income (F – C)	G	

Cash-Flow Projection Form

	Month												
	1st	2nd	3rd	4th	5th	6th	7th	8th	9th	10th	11th	12th	Total
1. Sales													
2. Cost of sales													
3. Gross profit													
EXPENSES													
4. Advertising													
5. Automobile													
6. Bank discounts													
7. Depreciation													
8. Dues & subscriptions													
9. Insurance													
10. Interest													
11. Office supplies													
12. Payroll taxes													
13. Professional services													
14. Rent													
15. Repairs & maintenance													
16. Salaries													
17. Supplies													
18. Taxes/licenses													
19. Utilities/phone													
20. Miscellaneous													
21. Total expenses													
22. Profit before taxes													

Cash-Flow Projection Form, continued

	1st	2nd	3rd	4th	5th	6th	7th	8th	9th	10th	11th	12th	Total
						Month							
INCOME													
23. Cash sales													
24. Accounts receivable													
25. Other													
26. Total cash available													
DISBURSEMENTS													
27. Owner's draw													
28. Loan repayment													
29. Cost of sales (line 2)													
30. Total expenses (less line 7)													
31. Capital expenditures													
32. Tax reserve													
33. Other													
34. Total disbursements													
35. Monthly cash flow													
36. Cumulative cash flow													

Balance Sheet

Name of Your Business

Date

ASSETS	LIABILITIES
Current assets	Current liabilities
Cash	Accounts payable
Accounts receivable	Accrued liabilities
Inventory	Taxes
Total Current Assets	Total Current Liabilities
Fixed assets	Long-term liabilities
Capital/plant	Bonds payable
Investment	Notes payable
Miscellaneous assets	Total Long-Term Liabilities
Total Fixed Assets	
TOTAL ASSETS	TOTAL LIABILITIES
	OWNER'S EQUITY/NET WORTH
	(total assets minus total liabilities)

Expense Report

Use this expense report to record expenses for traveling to trade shows, conventions, on buying trips, or just doing deliveries around the area.

Name _____ Start date _____

Purpose _____ End date _____

Date	Breakfast	Lunch	Dinner	Tips	Lodgings	Phone	Travel	Parking/Tolls	Gas/Oil	Entertainment	Miscellaneous	Daily Total

Subtotal	
Less Advance	
Total Amount Due	

Cost of Goods Sold—Merchandiser

(a) Cost of Goods Sold (Merchandiser)		
For Period Ending December 31, 2002		Totals
Net Sales		$
Beginning inventory, January 1, 2002	$	
Merchandise purchases	$	
Freight	$	
Cost of Goods Available for Sale		$
Less ending inventory, December 31, 2002	$	
Cost of Goods Sold		$

(b) Cost of Goods Manufactured		
For Period Ending December 31, 2002		Totals
Work in process inventory, January 1, 2002	$	
Inventory, January 1, 2002	$	
Purchases	$	
Freight in	$	
Cost of Materials Available for Use		$
Less inventory, December 31, 2002	$	
Cost of Materials Used		$
Direct Labor		$
Indirect labor	$	
Factory utilities	$	
Factory supplies used	$	
Insurance & taxes	$	
Depreciation	$	
Total Manufacturing Overhead		$
Total Manufacturing Costs		$
Total Work in Process During Period		$
Less work in process inventory, December 31, 2002	$	
Cost of Goods Manufactured		$

Appendix E
Business Strategy Forms

Prospecting Sheet

Most successful gift basket businesses court corporate clients for their large and somewhat regular orders. Use this form to keep track of any prospecting you do.

CLIENT INFORMATION   SEND MEDIA KIT ___

Company name		
Type of business		
Company address		
City	State	Zip
Telephone	Fax	
Contact	Title	
Decision maker	Title	

▲

GOALS OF THE CALL

GOALS OF THE CUSTOMER

WAYS TO HELP CUSTOMER FULFILL GOALS

OBJECTIONS OF CUSTOMER

RESPONSE TO OBJECTIONS

WAYS TO ENSURE CUSTOMER SATISFACTION

Competitive Analysis

It's critical to know who your competitors are and where you fall in the market compared to them. Use this worksheet to get a better handle on who is out there that you are competing with for the same market dollars.

A. Who are your three primary competitors?

1. _____

2. _____

3. _____

Describe each of them in terms of who their primary customers are, where the business is located, what their main market is, and what range the pricing of their gift baskets falls in.

1. _____

2. _____

3. _____

B. Who are your main secondary competitors?

1. _____

2. _____

3. _____

Describe them in the same terms as the primary competitors:

1. _____

2. _____

3. _____

What other businesses compete for your same customers? Determine whether the businesses can be complementary with yours or are strictly competitive. For instance, perhaps you sell cloth diapers and another business sells cleaning products for cloth diapers—that business could complement yours.

Appendix F
Self-Assessment

Thinking seriously ahead of time about whether you are suited for the gift basket business or suited for owning a business at all is time well spent. Many people are surprised at how much they loved their hobby and how unappealing it was after they made it into a business. Or how much they love doing the work but despise being tied to a retail shop. Asking yourself a few key questions can help you avoid some potential agony.

1. What are three things you really like to do and consider yourself good at:

   a. _____

   b. _____

   c. _____

2. What are three things you really don't like to do and know you are not good at:

   a. _____

   b. _____

   c. _____

3. List three things you enjoy about your current work:

a. _____

b. _____

c. _____

4. List three things you don't enjoy about your current work:

a. _____

b. _____

c. _____

5. If you could design your day any way you want, what would it be like?

_____

_____

_____

6. What are three things you would like to change about your current work?

a. _____

b. _____

c. _____

These questions are just the proverbial tip of the iceberg, but use them to get you thinking about your own life's goals and likes and dislikes.

Web Link Worksheet

A key way to drive customers to your website is to link with others—they put your website on their site and you put theirs on yours, with an easy hyperlink that allows customers to simply click on your website name and sends them to your site.

Use this worksheet not only to keep track of whom you are linking with, but also listing sites you would like to link with.

In the Notes section, comment on why you think this is a good site to link with, how successful it has been, and any agreements you made with the link partner (discounts on goods to each other, renewing your agreement every six months, that kind of thing). Make sure you note in the date section when the link started.

URL	Notes	Date Started
1.		
2.		
3.		
4.		
5.		
6.		
7.		
8.		
9.		
10.		

Focus Group Questionnaire

Focus groups are a great way to learn a lot about how to create the products that your target market wants to buy. You can use a focus group as a learning tool before you start your business or when you are looking to introduce a new basket or line of baskets. Pick a small (10–12) group of people in the demographic of your target buyer, gather in a comfortable, convenient, and private setting, order a couple pizzas, show some sample products/baskets, and ask some of the following types of questions:

Get a sense of their gift basket-buying history:

1. How many times a year do you purchase gift baskets?

2. What is the price range you look for in a gift basket?

3. Do you buy ready-made baskets or prefer custom-made ones?

4. What price range would you expect for a custom basket?

Show the samples you have brought. Allow the group members to open the sample baskets, and get a feel for what the recipient would experience receiving this basket. Then ask:

1. Are these baskets the level of quality you would be looking for?

2. Are they too large, too small, or just right?

3. Do they have a good number of items in them? Too sparse? Too cluttered?

4. What price would you expect to pay for these baskets?

5. Would you consider giving one of these baskets as a gift?

6. What do you think of the names these baskets have been given? (This discussion can be time- consuming!)

7. What other items or themes would be appealing to you in a gift basket of this size and price range?

Then find out something about delivery mechanisms:

1. Do you prefer to/typically buy your gift baskets locally and deliver them your-self?

2. Do you prefer to shop from your computer and look at baskets on a website?

3. Do you prefer your gift baskets delivered by common carrier or by a specialized delivery service?

Glossary

Accounts payable: The amount of money owed by a business for goods or services bought on credit.

Accounts receivable: The amount of money owed to a business for goods or services sold on credit.

Add-on selling: Encouraging customers to buy additional, related items; also referred to as suggestive selling and companion selling.

Aging: The length of time since an invoice was generated.

A la carte: Offering a selection of individual items that customers can pick and choose from to create a basket of their choice.

Americans with Disabilities Act (ADA): Federal law concerned with making public buildings and areas accessible to disabled people.

Anchoring: Securing items in a basket so that they are not tumbling around.

Better Business Bureau: A consumer watchdog organization that keeps tabs on businesses and their consumer relationships.

Business plan: A written document charting a business's mission, strategies, sales projections, and plan for growth. It is used to obtain financing and as a road map for growth.

Capital: Money invested in your business.

Cart: In retailing, a wheeled stand used to set up a temporary retail operation.

Cash flow: Money coming in and money going out of your business.

Cellophane: A thin, transparent, impermeable material made of cellulose used to wrap gift baskets and for other decorative purposes; comes in a variety of colors including clear.

C.O.D. (cash on delivery): Payment at the time the merchandise is delivered or picked up by the customer.

Companion selling: See Add-on selling.

Compiled list: A mailing list composed of people in specific categories, e.g., doctors, lawyers, San Francisco residents.

Cost of goods sold: The amount that the products, or the parts of the products, you sell cost to buy. Abbreviated as COGS.

Customer: The individual or company that orders and pays for the gift basket and other goods and services.

Customer profile: A record of a customer's preferences and purchases that help you customize baskets for them and recall their personal favorites, providing them with excellent customer service.

Customizing: Offering baskets done per order and items by request, opposed to premade baskets.

Dba: Fictitious business name, "doing business as."

Discount: The amount by which a price is reduced to create an incentive for various consumer behaviors, such as to increase sales or encourage early payment.

Distributorship: Selling another company's basket designs in your market area.

Drop ship: Having an order sent directly from the manufacturer or supplier to the customer.

First-in, first out (FIFO): An accounting system uses to value inventory for tax purposes. Under FIFO, inventory is valued at its most recent cost.

Focus group: A group of people gathered for the purpose of conducting market research.

Foot traffic: In retailing, the people walking by or in a store.

Franchise: A branch of a national chain of retail stores which you open and manage, are required to do things in the same way as all other branches, and give a certain percentage of profits back to the parent company.

Gondola: A type of display unit typically used in retail stores, usually a bank of freestanding shelves open on all sides; its primary function is to display goods and provide space for backup stock.

Heat gun: A handheld device that blows hot air and is used to seal or shrink plastic packaging materials.

Incentive gifts: Corporate programs for regular incentive gifting, such as "employee of the month" or "purchase XX and get a free gift basket."

Income statement: A report of all collections and disbursements for a business during a specific period, often monthly, used to determine net profit/loss.

Inventory turnover: A method whereby sales is divided by the capital invested in inventory, which helps evaluate how well the business owner is operating the business.

Keystone: To double the wholesale cost of an item when arriving at the retail price.

Kiosk: A lightly constructed, open booth often used by retailers in enclosed malls.

Last in, first out (LIFO): An accounting system for valuing inventory. Under LIFO, inventory is valued according to the remaining stock in inventory.

Line of credit: An agreement by the bank to lend a specified amount of money over a certain amount of time, usually one year.

Liquidity: How fast a business can convert assets to cash.

List broker: A company or individual specializing in mailing list rentals.

Loan origination fee: Percentage of a mortgage or other loan paid to the bank to be granted the loan.

Marking guns: Devices used to affix prices or bar codes to retail merchandise.

Market niche: The segment of a market in which you plan to excel.

Markup: The amount by which the wholesale price of an item is increased to reach the retail price.

▲

Media plan: A plan that details the usage of media in an advertising campaign including a budget, time span, markets, reach, frequency, rationales, and strategies.

Minimum: the amount that a supplier requires customers to order.

Nested baskets: Baskets of gradually increasing sizes nested in each other.

Net worth: A person or business's assets minus liabilities.

Outsource: The concept and process of hiring outside firms to provide products and services traditionally handled within a company.

Overhead: Ongoing administrative costs of the business that usually remain the same from month to month.

Poly bags: Clear, sometimes tinted, often sealable bags to hold small or individual items or to enclose the entire finished basket.

POS (point of sale): A term applied to events that happen as the sale is taking place (for example, a POS display is a display of merchandise adjacent to the checkout counter).

Pro forma: A projected sales estimate, like a "pro forma income statement."

Product: An item, like a completed gift basket, that a company manufactures or sells.

Rack: A floor stand for holding goods on shelves, on hooks, or in pockets.

Recipient: The individual who receives the gift basket; usually not the customer.

Response list: A mailing list composed of people who have previously responded to mail order campaigns.

Retail sales: Sales to the public.

Retailing: Selling to the public.

Roll-over service: A telephone feature that permits a busy line to roll over to another line.

Selects: Specific categories, such as age, location, or income bracket, by which names on a mailing list can be sorted and selected for mailings.

Shelf life: The length of time a product will keep without deterioration that makes it unsaleable; biggest concern with edible basket items.

Shred: The filler used to line the bottom of the basket. Can be paper, tissue, cellophane, even wood shavings. Comes in all manner of colors.

Shrink wrap: A plastic film used to wrap gift baskets; it shrinks to form a custom fit when heat is applied.

Shrinkage: A term used to describe losses when inventory is reduced by theft (either internally or externally) or errors.

SKU (stock keeping units): An inventory numbering system.

Step lease: A lease outlining annual increases in the tenant's base rent based on an approximation of what the lessor thinks expenses may be.

Suggestive selling: See Add-on selling.

Supplier: A company that sells goods and services to other companies.

Telecommunications device (TDD): A device that gives the hearing-impaired telephone access.

Trademark: Any word, name, symbol, or device, or any combination, used or intended to be used in commerce to identify and distinguish the goods of one manufacturer or seller from goods manufactured or sold by others, and to indicate the source of the goods.

Tulle: Netting used to make bows or wrap baskets, usually sold by the spool or the bolt.

Turn rate: The frequency that an inventory item, like a basket, turns over, or sells, in a year.

Vendor: Another term for supplier; less commonly used.

Wholesaling: Selling for resale.

Working capital: Net current assets required for the company to carry on its work; the surplus of a firm's current assets over its current liabilities.

Index

A

Accountant, 41, 42
Advertising, 115–116
  with complimentary
      baskets, 111–112
  (*See also* Marketing)
Advisory board, 43–45
All-nighter to fulfill last-minute
  corporate order, 12–13
Amateur to pro, 4, 142
Animal lovers, catering to, 22
Appendix A, Gift basket service
  resources, 147–150
Appendix B, Naming work-
  sheet, 151–152
Appendix C, Checklists, 153–
  164
Appendix D, Financial work-
  sheets, 165–173

Appendix E, Business strategy
  forms, 175–177
Appendix F, Self-assessment,
  179–182
Art of basket composition, 3–4,
  143–144
Attorney, 41

B

Banker, 42
Basket-assembling equipment,
  95
Best practices for small
  businesses, 5–6
Billing, 15, 133–134
Brochure, 71
  distribution, 111
  supplier's, 14
Burn out, avoiding, 9

Business
    card as marketing tool, 111, 144
    checking account and credit card, 56
    evaluation checklist, 157–158
    legal and ethical obligations of, 146
    opportunity, purchasing a, 77, 78, 80
    planning as crucial component of
        success, 9
Business plan, 48–51
    checklist, 163
Buying an existing operation, 76–77

C

Cart and kiosk rental, 67–68
Cash register, 94
Catalog, 71
    supplier's, 14
Checklists, 153–164
Cold calling, 112
Competition
    differentiating yourself from the,
        28–29
    stealing ideas from the, 142
Competitive analysis, 177
Complimentary baskets as promotional
    tool, 111–112, 119–120
Computer expert, 43
Consignment sales, 73–74
Consultants, 43
Containers
    as keepsake, 7
    beyond baskets, 100
Corporate sector
    catering to, 114
    customer prospecting sheet, 175–
        176
    defining segments of broad market,
        25
    growth of, 21–22
    phone sales, 24
    selling to, 23–24
Cost per basket, 56

Costs of goods sold, sample, 99
Credit
    and collection policies, 134–137
    and debit card processing
        equipment, 95
    and debit cards, accepting, 136–137
    application, sample, 139–140
    establishing and maintaining your
        own flawless, 145
Customer
    "love letters," 142
    accessibility, 143
    business, 23–24, 25
    credit, 134–137
    feedback, 145
    focus group questionnaire, 182
    guarantee, 145
    individual, 22–23
    information questionnaire, sample,
        163
    marketing letter, sample, 113
    personal shopping service, 145
    profiles and order information, 13,
        17–18
    referrals, 112
    relationships, building, 14
    service as marketing tool, 111
    target, 14, 19
    thank-you-for-your-time basket to
        corporate, 24
    word-of-mouth, 112, 116, 144
Customized baskets, 13, 28, 101
Cyberspace
    don't avoid, 130
    selling in, 121–130 (See also Website)

D

Delivery deadline, importance of honor-
    ing, 16
Direct-mail
    advertising, 115–116
    pieces, 71

Directory advertising, 116
Displays, 74–75
Don't market by price, 144

E

E-mail etiquette, 129
E-newsletter, 128
eBay, 126–127
Employees, 81–88
    benefits, insurance and labor laws,
        86, 87–88
    finding and hiring, 83–85
    interviewing and evaluating
        potential, 84–85
    pay scale, 83
    temporary, 13
    training, 85–87
Equipment, 89–107
    checklist, 96–97
    documenting your, 56
Equipping your business, 89–107
Existing resources, checklist for, 157
Extras, enhancing your gift baskets with,
    145

F

Failure, reasons for small business,
    8–9
Fairs, 68–69
Festivals, 68–69
Finances, 47–60
Financial
    management, 131–146
    record keeping, 133
    statements, 132–133, 138
    worksheets, 165–173
Financing, 51–52
Flea markets, 68–69
Focus group questionnaire, 182
Food
    and scented personal products, rule
        of no mixing, 15

baskets, gourmet, 26
    items, FDA and health department
        regulations, 98, 146
Franchise, pros and cons of purchasing,
    77–80
Freight costs, 43, 45–46
Full-time enterprise, 7

G

Giftware, 4
Giving yourself a boost when you need
    it, 142
Glossary, 183–187
Gourmet/food baskets, 26

H

Holiday-based business, 2
Holidays, targeting lesser-known, 115
Homebased business, 61–62, 69–70
    tax advantages, 69–70
    zoning codes, 70
Hours, business, 11–12

I

Income potential, 2, 13
Incorporating, 38
Insurance, 40
    agent, 41–42
    planning checklist, 161
Internet sales, 121–130. *See also* Website
Inventory, 98, 100–105
    checklist, 103
    control, 103–105
    excess, 105
    tracking, 105
Invoicing, 15, 133–134

K

Kiosk rental, 67–68

L

Labels, custom, 114
Labor costs, 56
Lead times, 104–105

Learning opportunities, 142–143
Lease
    checklist, 160
    terms, 66–67
Legal/ownership structure of business, 37–39
Licenses and permits, 38–39
Locating and setting up your business, 61–80
Location checklist, 156

M
Mail order business, 71, 73
Mailing lists, 71–72
Management and administration, 12
Manufacturers' representatives, relationships with, 14–15
Market
    defining your, 21–32
    planning checklist, 155
    research, 22–23
    survey, 31
Marketing
    details, 16, 19
    ongoing, 144
    plan, 110–111, 144
    to basket recipients, sample customer letter, 113–114
    your business, 12, 109–120
Marketplace visibility, 114
Merchandise
    displaying, 74–75
    marts, 15
Mission statement, 29–30
    worksheet, 32
Mistakes, learning from your, 143

N
Naming
    your baskets, 119
    your company, 34–35, 151–152
Niche
    choosing your, 14, 24–25
    market worksheet, 27

O
Occasions, gift basket giving, 3
Office equipment, 90–94, 102
Online sales, 121–130. *See also* Website
Operations, 11–19
Order taking, 13
Outdoor events, 68–69
Outsourcing trend, 15–16
Overlap, avoiding, 24
Overview, industry, 1–9

P
Packaging, 46, 101
Packing and shipping tips, 72, 104
Partnership, 38
Personal care products, 4
Phone sales, 24
Playing by the rules, 146
Presentation, 3–4
Pricing, 54–55, 144
    checklist, 161
Product line, 26, 28, 104
Production, 12–13
    area, 75
Professional services, 41–43
Profits, 13
Public relations and promotions, 119–120
Purchasing, 13–15, 98–104. *See also* Inventory, Suppliers

R
Record keeping, 54–56
Referrals, rewarding, 112
Resources, gift basket service, 147–150
Retail store location, 62–67

S
Sales representatives, relationships with, 14–15
Sales tax, 134

Security, workplace, 106–107
Self assessment, is the gift basket business for you?, 179–180
Selling in cyberspace, 121–130
Shipping
    and receiving, 45–46
    supplies, 46
Shower baskets, 26, 28
Sole proprietorship, 37
Special purchases, 103
Specialty food, 4
Standard baskets, 28
Startup
    budget, 52–54
    capital, 5
    expenses worksheet, 59–60
    expenses, estimated, 57–58
    funds, sources of, 51–52, 53–54
    SBA loans, 53–54
    stories, 6–8
Staying focused and organized, 144–145
Structuring your business, 33–46
Subscriptions to industry-specific and general business publications, 143
Success and failure, stories of, 141–146
Suppliers, 13–15, 98–103
    establishing and maintaining flawless credit with, 145
    payment terms and credit policies, 137, 139–140
Survey, market research, 31
SWOT Analysis, 50–51

T

Taking their breath away, 143–144
Taking yourself and your business seriously, 142
Tales from the trenches, 141–146
Taxes, 134, 136, 146
Telecommunications equipment, 92–94
Theme and contents, coordinating, 4

Time off for you, 82
Toiletry baskets, 26
Trade and bartering arrangements, 146
Trade shows, 15, 100–102, 116–119
    exercising caution at, 15
    exhibit do's and don'ts, 117
    tips for, 100, 102
Trademarks, 36–37
Trends, tracking, 153–154
Turning pro, 54–56, 142
Types of baskets, 26, 28

V

Vacations, 82
Vehicles, company, 106
Visual impact of basket, 3–4, 143–144
Visual merchandising, 74–75

W

Warehouse/light industrial space, 73
Website
    "clicks" and tips for attracting visitors and buyers, 128
    "drilling down," 124
    company, 72, 121–130
    design, 123–124
    e-mail newsletter, 128
    linking and selling through other sites, 127, 181
    marketing your, 127–128
    payment options, 126
    set-up, 122–123
    shopping cart, 125
    usability and stickiness, 129
Word-of-mouth marketing, 112, 116, 144
Work area, 75

Y

Yellow Pages advertising, 116